FAVOURITE NIGHTS

&

CAUGHT ON A TRAIN

by

STEPHEN POLIAKOFF

A Methuen New Theatrescript
Methuen · London

A Methuen Paperback

First published in 1982 by Methuen London Ltd., 11 New Fetter Lane,
London EC4P 4EE
Copyright © 1982 by Stephen Poliakoff

Set in 10pt IBM Press Roman by 𝍏 Tek-Art, Croydon, Surrey
Printed in Great Britain by Richard Clay (The Chaucer Press) Ltd, Bungay, Suffolk

ISBN 0 413 50100 0

CAUTION
All rights whatsoever in these plays are strictly reserved and application for
performance etc., should be made to Margaret Ramsay Ltd., 14a Goodwin's Court,
St. Martin's Lane, London WC2N 4LL. No performance may be given unless a
licence has been obtained.

FAVOURITE NIGHTS
& CAUGHT ON A TRAIN

This double Poliakoff volume contains his most recent stage play, *Favourite Nights,* which opened at the Lyric, Hammersmith, in November 1981, and the full screenplay of *Caught on a Train,* the television film starring Peggy Ashcroft which won the 1981 BAFTA award for Best Single Play, as well as the Television Critics' Best Play Award, and was the BBC-TV's entry for the Prix Italia.

'Poliakoff makes us look afresh at the everyday tat of our civilisation and recognise the extreme weirdness of it all . . . A revolving high-rise restaurant, plush public furniture nailed to the floor, multi-coloured cocktails, a rubber plant turned yellowish by hastily disposed-of alcohol, constant musak: much that obviously fascinates Poliakoff the anthropologist is invoked or shown in *Favourite Nights* itself. The play starts in a singularly charmless hotel foyer, but its geographic centre is what, on bad days, seems to me the spiritual centre of our culture. It's set in a casino, complete with roulette and blackjack tables, mushroom-faced croupiers, cameras perpetually scanning the punters.'

Benedict Nightingale, *New Statesman*

'*Caught On A Train* is recognisably in the train film genre; young man in trans-continental express, unsettled by high-handed old lady and more or less hostile passengers . . . Hitchcock out of Kafka. And it certainly winds up the suspense, with inventive plotting from Poliakoff.'

Peter Fiddick, *Guardian*

'One of the most impressive ventures of the television year.'

Herbert Kretzmer, *Daily Mail*

Front cover photos: the photograph of Peggy Ashcroft as Frau Messner in Caught On A Train *is reproduced by courtesy of the BBC; the photograph of Susan Tracy as Catherine in the Lyric Theatre Hammersmith production of* Favourite Nights *is reproduced by courtesy of Donald Cooper.*

by Stephen Poliakoff

AMERICAN DAYS
HITTING TOWN & CITY SUGAR
SHOUT ACROSS THE RIVER
STRAWBERRY FIELDS
THE SUMMER PARTY

FAVOURITE NIGHTS

Favourite Nights was first presented at the Lyric Theatre, Hammersmith, on 2 November 1981, with the following cast:

CATHERINE	Susan Tracy
LANGER	Peter Postlethwaite
SARAH	Gwyneth Strong
MR MICHAELS	Martin Friend
ALAN	John Duttine
GIRL	Marion Bailey
AMERICAN	Peter Banks

Directed by Peter James
Designed by Grant Hicks
Lighting by Mick Hughes

The set should be suggestive of an overall faded West End red — simple and uncluttered, allowing the scenes to slide at each other.

ACT ONE

Scene One

The sun streams in. There is a plain table and two rather battered-looking chairs and a stool in the room. On the table there are three books, a tape-recorder and a large empty ashtray. On the wall, the same dark faded-plush red as the rest of the set, there are one or two postcards of desert sunsets, the Pyramids and New York. There is also a clock which has stopped at twelve.

It is a hot summer's day. Langer, a large man of thirty-eight, is sitting on the chair a little way from the table. He is over-weight and looks old for his age. But he has a very prosperous appearance, in a perfectly fitting electric blue suit. He speaks with an Austrian accent.

Catherine is standing with her back to the sunlight, facing him. She is in her late twenties, a tall woman, with long hair, striking looking without being conventionally pretty. She has a very open, direct smile. She has a North London accent.

As she faces Langer, he is perched on a chair which is much too small for him. He dwarfs it. Langer is calmly wiping his forehead. Catherine watches him, and then speaks to him, firmly, but quietly.

CATHERINE. Tell me when you're ready to go on . . .

LANGER. A moment, please . . .

He finishes wiping and, stretching out his legs, folds his arms and looks straight back at her.

Right . . .

CATHERINE. Are you sure you're

comfortable like that? You can take your jacket off you know.

LANGER. No — it is fine. The day is hotter than it was going to be. (*He looks at her.*) And you are dressed for it and I am not. You have no air-conditioning here, but I will be fine. So . . . I will tell you about my hotel now. (*He begins loudly.*) — The beds . . . are very small, I have two of them, two beds, side by side.

CATHERINE. Side by side.

LANGER. And when you climb into them . . . they slide, like that . . . (*He demonstrates with his hand.*) They slide along the ground. And they are extremely hard, stiff, like in a boys' school. (*Pause.*) I hardly fit into the bed, in fact . . . you know. (*He smiles.*) They must be used to smaller men. (*Pause.*) I am seeing if you are going to stop me . . . but I haven't made a mistake. (*Pause.*) The room is very large, my room, but the curtains are so heavy . . . you cannot move them by hand. And they are stuck — half-open and half-shut across the window. However hard you pull and tear them, they do not move. So my room is in darkness.

CATHERINE. That's good. Quite good. Go on.

LANGER. And you can hear the water coming from the radiator, you are lying there, just near falling into sleep . . . and you hear it first from a long way, moving towards you, and then slowly, slowly, it gets *louder*, and the radiator . . . the radiator starts shaking and jumping, it gets very excited, and makes a noise like this, which you cannot stop, like this . . .

He makes a rattling noise on the table.

CATHERINE. OK, I think we can leave the radiator and move on . . .

LANGER. And the colour television — there is a picture but no sound. (*He smiles.*) and the person next door . . . he . . . he . . .

CATHERINE (*watching him*): He sings

before he goes to bed, and hurls his shoes around.

LANGER (*surprised, looks up*): Yes . . . you're right. It is expensive of course, the hotel. Because of my company, the business, I always try to stay in the best hotels, one of the two or three best in each city.

Pause. He smiles straight at her.

But generally it is fine, the hotel.

CATHERINE. Yes . . . it sounds fairly reasonable. That was good.

Langer stares at her confidently.

LANGER. I know.

CATHERINE. But turn your book over. Go on.

Langer looks down at the text-book.

You keep on giving it a furtive little glance.

LANGER. There is nothing helping me in this book . . .

CATHERINE. Go on, turn it over. You really don't need it you know. You've got to be able to manage without it.

LANGER. I am. (*With an abrupt movement he turns the book over.*)

CATHERINE (*indicating the book*): What is that part of the book called?

LANGER. The bone.

CATHERINE. The spine.

LANGER (*staring straight at her*): Spines.

He stares at her confidently.

CATHERINE. Now, tell me what you're wearing.

LANGER (*reels it off, very fast, as if he has been expecting it*): I am wearing a blue suit, made in Brussels, my socks are blue, and the shirt is blue, very good quality, very good shop in Frankfurt . . . and black shoes which are English, shoes are very important in a foreign city.

Silence. Langer stares at her confidently.

CATHERINE. I didn't understand a word of that.

LANGER. You must have understood some of it . . .

CATHERINE (*calmly*): You are not allowed, as you know full well, to learn things off by heart. And *I* should never ask the same question twice.

LANGER. I remembered from last time.

CATHERINE. So I see.

LANGER (*smiles at her smugly*): One of the men in my company, a junior executive, has been to this school too, he was also asked to talk about his clothes all the time, every lesson they asked him the same things! And he told me . . . so I knew what to expect even then.

CATHERINE (*slight smile*): I'm glad to see you discuss the course before you get here.

Slight pause.

LANGER. Oh yes.

Sarah enters, a girl of twenty-one, short hair, sharp features, tidily dressed, summer clothes, bare arms, she has a shoulder bag. She has a North London accent. Her manner is impulsive, but shy. She stands in the entrance.

CATHERINE. Sarah — it's you already.

SARAH. That's right. Do I come in or go . . . or just loiter in the doorway.

CATHERINE. No, come in.

SARAH (*quite nervously as she moves into the teaching area*): Walking up the stairs, there are all these strange noises coming from behind each doorway. I had to stand still on the landing and listen for yours . . .

CATHERINE (*calmly cuts her off*): We're in the middle of a lesson, so you can only stay if you are going to be quiet — and also try to keep still. You'll have to squat on that.

Catherine indicates the stool. She ruffles Sarah's hair, a casual, but warm greeting.

SARAH. Yes . . .

She sits on the stool, watchfully, and remains fairly still throughout the rest of the scene.

CATHERINE (*gently*): And don't talk . . .

Catherine turns back and looks at Langer.

LANGER. Aren't you going to introduce us?

CATHERINE. No. Afterwards, maybe. Now . . .

LANGER. You want me to go on with her watching?! It is not possible.

CATHERINE. Of course it is.

Slight pause.

LANGER. Your clock has stopped.

CATHERINE (*slight smile*): I know — I keep it stopped, it prevents people glancing up at it every other moment, urging it on.

LANGER. But I have another check, you see . . .

He takes out a wrist watch from his jacket pocket.

CATHERINE (*slight smile*): You've smuggled one in, have you?

Slight pause.

Give me your watch.

LANGER (*surprised*): Give it to you . . .

CATHERINE (*calmly*): No come on. One of the house rules. (*She smiles calmly.*) I don't allow watches. Come on, hand it over . . . it will be perfectly safe with me.

LANGER (*very dubious, hands it over*): Here . . . careful, it is a very expensive one, high quality.

Catherine takes the watch and puts it in a drawer in the table.

LANGER. Why, you put it in the drawer?

CATHERINE. Don't worry, it'll survive. Right . . .

LANGER (*shifting on the small chair*): It it so small, these places, these rooms.

We will all be squashed, suffocate.

CATHERINE. That's perfectly possible.

LANGER. You will be responsible.

CATHERINE. When the place was really busy — until recently — completely bulging with pupils, the rooms would shrink every day, a beaming head would appear above the door, 'Just got to move your wall a few feet today,' and it would come squeaking towards you across the floor — and stop just inches away from the pupil's head. It occasionally shaved a few ears off.

She stops, and looks immediately to see if Langer is watching her.

CATHERINE. What did the walls do . . .?

LANGER. I understand . . . I understand. They came towards you.

CATHERINE (*slight smile*): I should warn you, I'm very good at telling when people are not attending — they stare at you extremely intently, straight into your eyes . . .

Langer is sitting upright, staring at her:

and nod at very regular intervals.

LANGER. It is after lunch that it is *really* difficult to concentrate. (*Langer glances at the clock.*)

CATHERINE. It is still stopped.

LANGER. I know. I was just hoping. (*He looks at her.*) I am not the worst pupil you've had I'm sure . . . I'm not . . . am I?

CATHERINE. Trying to distract me into doing the talking can be an unwise tactic.

Silence. She stares at Langer.

I had an Italian, a young industrialist, two weeks ago, who was the worst. Every morning he came in here and put his legs on the table, showing off his very brown ankles, he was obviously quite proud of them; he always had sleep in his eyes, regardless of the time of day, and he used to pick it very delicately out of the corner of his eye, drop it into his palm, and then eat it, very slowly, like he was savouring cocktail morsels, parma ham. (*She turns instantly to Langer.*) What did he do?

LANGER. He . . . he put his legs on the table . . . You see I was following.

CATHERINE (*watching Langer*): But some of them work extremely hard, take their books back to their hotel rooms.

LANGER. It is lucky you don't have a window with a view. I would stare out all the time . . .

CATHERINE. I used to have a classroom on the street, but bits of the West End used to be flicked through the windows all day, lighted cigarettes, parking tickets, choc-ices, guitar strings . . .

She stops, and half turns, but Langer is immediately replying.

LANGER. No, no . . . You don't have to ask, I will tell you — through the window you got . . .

CATHERINE (*stopping him*): I will let you off that one. Now . . . I want you to answer these questions as quickly as you can. (*Calmly.*) Where did you buy that magazine in your pocket?

LANGER (*shifts uneasily*): Which magazine?

CATHERINE (*lightly*): Have you got more than one magazine in your pocket?

LANGER. I bought it . . . at the airport.

CATHERINE. And what is the magazine about?

LANGER. It is not what you are thinking it is.

CATHERINE. What do I think it is?

LANGER. . . . You think it is . . . I'm not so good at doing this quickly . . . a magazine for the men.

CATHERINE (*smiles gently*): No such thought crossed my mind I assure you. Are you going to tell me about it?

LANGER. Yes . . . it is only . . . wait a moment . . . (*He pulls at magazine in his pocket, we do not know if he is concealing another.*) a magazine about aircraft.

CATHERINE. And what else have you bought in England — *that you can tell me about*?!

LANGER. Yes, I . . . I find this difficult doing it so quickly.

CATHERINE (*lightly*): You want to learn English, don't you. You can do it . . . you've been doing very well this morning . . . so far.

LANGER. I . . . (*Suddenly floundering, lowers his head.*)

CATHERINE. Where you going? You haven't got a phrase book under there? Sometimes people disappear under the table, and then re-surface grinning all over their faces, they have this really small crib book, size of matchboxes, which they get off their sons, and which they can hide in their turn-ups.

LANGER. No, no. Just wait a moment. (*He is in much discomfort. He stands up.*) I think unfortunately . . . (*He takes his pristine suit jacket off, a red biro has exploded in his pocket staining his shirt, a furiously messy stain. Deeply embarrassed.*) The pen has burst . . . (*He takes it out of his pocket, it is spreading its sticky ink.*) It is very untidy, I am sorry . . . (*He doesn't know where to put the pen.*) I don't want to get it on my books . . .

CATHERINE. Don't worry, here —

She takes a towel out of the drawer in the desk.

SARAH (*surprised*): You keep one handy for all of them, do you . . .?

LANGER. I have never done this before, at school my desk was usually clean.

SARAH. I was always doing it.

CATHERINE (*watching Langer, lightly*): It is very mucky . . .

Sarah resumes her still position, watching Catherine's authority.

LANGER. I have made a terrible mess, I'm sorry . . . (*He looks at her, his composure returning.*) Maybe I should wash.

CATHERINE. No, we'll finish the lesson first. (*Lightly:*) You can clean your hands later. Now, read me what you have brought me.

Langer is surprised, tries to sidetrack her.

LANGER. I need a drink.

CATHERINE. You can have a drink later. (*Lightly:*) Remember, I decide when the lesson ends.

LANGER. No, no, you take me wrong. I don't want it to end. (*He looks down at his exercise book.*) This is my worst . . . I find writing English so difficult. (*He immediately starts to try to read his own writing.*) Before the opening of the new industrial s. . .site, we had to reduce the work force . . . these meant I had to dismiss at least thirty men, I had to dismiss, I had to dismiss them while we were still . . . no, dismiss them . . . (*He tails off.*)

CATHERINE. Can I see? (*She looks down at the paper.*) How long did you take to do this? You have written three different versions for each word.

LANGER. Please, you have me at my worst, having to read my writing . . . I look very desperately at the sides of buses trying to save up words, remember how to spell them —

CATHERINE (*lightly*): Your writing will be full of Red Rover ticket advertisements then. (*Looking at paper.*) And what on earth is this, is this a picture of me?

Langer tries to take it back.

LANGER (*he smiles, slightly lewdly*): I am not good at this, it is the thing I fear worst. (*He suddenly looks at her.*) I can tell you what you are wearing though, a skirt and a white blouse. Yesterday you were wearing red and black, with white and black buttons.

And green shoes, And you had a very large bracelet on . . .

CATHERINE. You're wrong about the very large bracelet. I don't have one.

LANGER. I'm not wrong. (*Pause.*) My head is like a balloon now. I am not allowed to smoke still?

CATHERINE. Not till you're outside, no.

LANGER. But I am a *smoker*. (*He smiles at Sarah.*) The taste in the mouth when you need one, you know at school in the end of the lesson, counting the moment till you could run down the street and puff, and you start using your pencil like this as a cigarette. All the boys towards the end of the lesson doing this, holding it like this, smoking their pencils. (*He laughs, slowly recovering his confidence.*)

CATHERINE (*quiet*): You'll have to do that now . . .

She tears up his copying exercise.

You know you are improving — but only just, a very slight creeping improvement.

LANGER. I know . . . I know. I *try*.

CATHERINE. Sometimes that is far from obvious.

Pause.

LANGER. I'm sorry. You are a remarkable teacher, you know . . . When I saw these schools, these mysterious places, with names like the Julius Caesar School of English, and these important businessmen disappearing inside, I wondered what went on, shut up there, who were the people that ran it.

CATHERINE (*lightly*): You're just beginning to find out . . .

LANGER. I walk here on the first day, what will my teacher look like, will she have spots, will she be a woman of fifty and built like a truck, and shout and stamp her foot?

CATHERINE. And you found she was all of those things. Maybe some shouting will be required next time . . .

LANGER. Please no . . . (*He looks at her.*) I had a teacher when I was small, she would dress, the word is, not like you . . . show her body . . .

CATHERINE. Daringly.

LANGER. Daringly. (*He looks at her.*) But she didn't seem to realise the effect she had. (*He looks at her again.*) She was very strict, but very popular. I was afraid of her. But I wanted to keep her with me, as I went up the school, grade by grade. Keep her along with me. We used to make this noise, us boys, when she came into the class, on the backs of our hands this noise, all of us. (*He does it.*)

CATHERINE. Squelching noise.

LANGER. She had a walk between the desks, like this, like a snake. (*He shows a zig-zag.*) I didn't expect to find somebody there like that. And I had a surprise coming in here too.

CATHERINE. You're suddenly extremely talkative — why aren't you like this the whole lesson?

LANGER. I will do better tonight. The things I would like to do . . . if I can . . . is the theatre, you have to, it is booked already, and also visit the Playboy Club, or gaming place, see some of the real West End.

CATHERINE. They often want to do that.

LANGER (*glancing at Sarah*): And also find out about you and your family.

CATHERINE. We'll have to see. But of course if you don't try, or if you're lazy, there's absolutely no point.

LANGER (*tone suddenly authoritative*): But you have to. (*Pause.*) I asked for it.

CATHERINE. Yes.

With a swift movement, she moves the clock on one hour.

Alright, you can go now.

He goes.

SARAH. At last! (*She leaps forward, having remained so still.*) My bum was getting destroyed by that bleeding stool! (*She stops, moves slightly nervously to kiss Catherine.*) I kept really still, didn't I? Hello Catherine.

They kiss, Sarah slightly nervously.

You look so well..You look terrific like that.

CATHERINE (*slight smile*): Untrue, I don't. Well tell me then?

SARAH. What?

CATHERINE. Your *results.* What else do you think . . .?

SARAH. *They haven't come out yet!* I must say — you're so cool. You can sit there calmly and wait to ask me to the end of the bloody lesson!

CATHERINE. What happens if they'd been bad, you wouldn't have wanted our city friend watching.

SARAH. No. I'm trying not to think about it, anyway. (*Slight pause.*) Not successfully. I think about it the whole fucking time. Christ, I've been sitting still so long I just (*She bounces round the room.*) got to get rid of it. (*She smiles.*) All of it.

CATHERINE. You'll have to make a mammoth effort and try not to worry.

SARAH (*she smiles*): I'm like this. (*She clenches her hand.*) . . . In the pit of my stomach: like volcanic jelly.

CATHERINE (*smiles at this*): Come on . . . (*She takes Sarah by the arm.*)

SARAH (*lets out a sudden shriek of pain*): Mind! Sorry, but you can't touch that. (*She gingerly moves her arm.*) I got sunburn, have to be careful, I tried to get brown when the exams were finished, and got toasted pink instead. It's incredibly painful, even where I didn't have bare flesh, it just went straight through my clothes as well! I can't get brown like you.

Sarah looks at Catherine, suddenly a bit shy of her again.

I haven't seen you for ages anyway.

CATHERINE. Three months.

SARAH. And that was only for a quarter of an hour in a café.

CATHERINE. Well, if you decide to go to a polytechnic all that way away . . .

SARAH. It's because it had good courses.

CATHERINE. I know.

SARAH. I'm here now. We're not rid of him then − the business man?

CATHERINE. Don't worry about that.

SARAH. You were really good with him. I like your hair like that.

CATHERINE. You've got to enjoy yourself now, somehow.

SARAH. I know − but I've got to take you to see Dad first.

Blackout.

Scene Two

Against the plush red fittings of the basic set are two plush armchairs, or an armchair and a wall seat, a potted bush as found in the foyers of hotels, and a silver ashtray.

In the armchair sits Mr Michaels, a man in his seventies. He is wearing tinted glasses and staring straight ahead. Musak is playing loudly at the start of the scene, but dips away, only to rise and fall again when we don't expect it.

Catherine and Sarah enter as the musak plays in the background. They stand for a second, side by side, staring across the stage at him.

CATHERINE. What's he doing wearing tinted glasses?

SARAH. He's started wearing them when he goes out. You gave them to him . . . don't you remember?

The two girls move up to him. Catherine stands behind his chair.

Who do you think I've brought to see you . . .?

MR MICHAELS. Who? (*He takes off his spectacles.*) Where . . .? It's you Catherine. (*His manner is by turns hazy with old age, and suddenly very sharp.*)

CATHERINE. Of course not! You look very comfortable down there . . . (*She kisses him on the cheek.*) Been stuffing yourself with olives have you?

MR MICHAELS (*cutting this off*): Have you heard anything yet?

SARAH. Since I left you here! How could I . . .?

MR MICHAELS (*turning to Catherine*): Has she heard anything − you'll give me an honest answer.

CATHERINE (*slight smile*): She's far more honest than I am! She hasn't heard anything.

SARAH. The moment I hear, I promise I will tell you.

MR MICHAELS. You'll find out now

before you leave here. I came down for a celebratory drink with you after all, so . . .

CATHERINE (*intervening effortlessly*): They have these enormous thick carpets here, have you noticed. This is the hotel of the purring carpets, late at night, when the place is empty there is this deep satisfied purr going round the whole building. And if you give it a gentle rub with your foot, the purr grows louder.

SARAH (*slight smile*): You come here often do you?

CATHERINE. This is also — you'll be pleased to hear — the hotel of the most superstitious lifts in London. They not only miss out the thirteenth floor, they don't have a floor nine either. It is to keep them safe from bomb blasts and visiting football teams.

MR MICHAELS (*indicating Catherine*): Surprised she has time to see me.

CATHERINE. What was that croak about. (*She puts her hand in the bag.*) I have brought you something very small. (*She pulls a parcel out of her bag, gift-wrapped with a shiny bow.*) Are you going to unwrap it or am I? You've got a very effective technique for opening parcels haven't you?

Mr Michaels rips open the parcel, tearing the paper in all directions.

(*Gently.*) Some more silk pyjamas — to make you look like Cary Grant.

SARAH. He's drowning in silk underwear from you already. His room is completely crammed with it.

MR MICHAELS (*staring at them*): Will they fit me? Must have cost a lot.

CATHERINE (*to Sarah*): Go and get us some cocktails. They are rather special here. You'll see why.

SARAH. What do I ask them for? Can I have one of your specials?

CATHERINE. Just choose.

Sarah goes.

MR MICHAELS (*looking down at his present*): I can't try them on here.

CATHERINE. I forgot . . . there is this as well. (*She takes out another small parcel which he rips open.*) It's a musical alarm clock, in fact there are a few things I've forgotten.

MR MICHAELS. Fishing things out of your stocking for me?

Some articles are gift-wrapped, others are not.

CATHERINE. Some exciting socks, some male perfume . . . an obscene amount of liqueur chocolates which will probably dribble all over the place, and some . . .

He rips open the paper impatiently.

(*Slight smile.*) It's a unique sight watching you open presents. You disembowel them.

MR MICHAELS. So many of them.

CATHERINE. They've been stockpiling because I haven't seen you for a little while. (*She smiles.*) Don't expect this much again.

Mr Michaels is sitting in a sea of torn wrapping paper.

Sarah enters with the drinks. Three enormous bright blue cocktails on a tray. She stands there with the drinks.

SARAH. Did I get the right ones?

CATHERINE (*looking at the blue drinks*): Almost.

MR MICHAELS. What have you put in these. (*To Catherine:*) What has she dropped in them?

SARAH. These are the most expensive drinks I've ever had: and these were the cheapest too. Each sip is costing you fifty pence.

CATHERINE. Late at night you can see these call girls bent over green and pink drinks by the bar, waiting and waiting.

SARAH (*looking down at the presents on the father's lap*): Are these some more things she's given you then? They seem to have multiplied while I've been out of the room. She spends such a lot on you doesn't she?

MR MICHAELS (*sharp*): Did you phone for your results when you went for the drinks?

SARAH (*taken aback*): No of course I didn't.

MR MICHAELS (*pushing the wrapping paper off his legs*): Where to put these. I have nowhere to put this. (*He indicates Catherine.*) She always makes me meet her in public places.

SARAH. Yes. You've met him in all sorts of bizarre places haven't you?

CATHERINE. Several times in the tea rooms at Selfridges, haven't we, the zoo . . .

MR MICHAELS. And in a revolving restaurant up a tower.

CATHERINE. Yes that squealed didn't it, remember it screeched with effort as it tried to go round.

MR MICHAELS. She pulls me up and down escalators . . . in these public places.

SARAH (*watching her*): Why do you always meet him in hotels?

MR MICHAELS. Is she going to phone? Please phone and find out if they've heard anything now.

SARAH (*loud*): Dad, I'm asking you please, don't go on about it.

MR MICHAELS. I need to know. If you just . . .

CATHERINE (*cutting him off, effortlessly*): And you always sit by the bushes in the hotels where we meet, don't you, and always too near the ashtrays, that's why you get covered in things.

MR MICHAELS. I can't walk far.

CATHERINE. Now stop playing the invalid. You look very well. Are you? (*Pause. Sharp.*) Now look at me, come on. (*To Sarah:*) His eye are wandering again. (*Back to Michaels:*) You're not watching television are you?

SARAH. Yes, I expect he is.

CATHERINE (*gently*): I have no idea how he always spots the televisions in these places, but he always smells them out, through doors, down passages — don't you?

Mr Michaels doesn't react.

SARAH. I never know how much he takes in of everything now, or how much he just chooses to ignore things.

MR MICHAELS (*suddenly*): What rubbish she's saying. I never watch the television!

Both girls look at him. Silence.

MR MICHAELS (*to Catherine*): I've been waiting to see you for so long, how many months . . .

CATHERINE. Not that long.

MR MICHAELS. And now I'm only going to get a few minutes! She never writes to me, do you know that?

SARAH. *I* write to you.

MR MICHAELS. You're *always* writing to me. (*He indicates Catherine.*) But she never writes to me, when she was abroad, months went by and not a word, she was all over the world and not one sound out of her. And then suddenly all at once I would get ten postcards, on the same day.

SARAH. That's right; made me read them to you.

MR MICHAELS (*suddenly at her*): Go over to the phone and give them a call, while I watch . . .

SARAH. I asked you not to Dad . . .

CATHERINE (*to her father*): Now if you're going to keep yelling about that, we'll have to leave you won't we, and you can shout it out to an empty hotel.

MR MICHAELS (*undeterred*): I can't understand why they are taking so long to mark them, do you understand that?

SARAH. You'll be the first to know. We may end up fighting about this, Dad.

CATHERINE (*to Sarah*): Don't worry. (*To Mr Michaels, severely*:) Now finish your drink.

MR MICHAELS. You're trying to stop me talking about her.

CATHERINE (*smiles,distracting him effortlessly*): Have a look at this now. (*She shows him the gold medallion round her neck.*)

SARAH (*quietly*): You handle him so much better than I do.

MR MICHAELS (*touches it*): That's a nice little article, who gave you that?

CATHERINE. I bought it. When you walk through the lobby of a hotel like this, or the Kensington Hilton, suddenly a hand'll stick out, and grab the chain, and you're yanked forward, being throttled. (*She shows, pulling the gold medallion.*) And these strange creatures loom out of the dark, the old American ladies, who shelter in the shadows here. 'Can I just have a look at that, dear,' and they hold on to you like you're a dog, while they twist it round to see if it's real gold! (*She glances round.*) If you look around these big hotel lobbies, it's full of them.

SARAH. You know so much about the West End now, don't you?

CATHERINE. Yes. You can meet a lot of strange people in places like this. (*Gently to her father*:) Like you.

MR MICHAELS. They nail the chairs to the floor now, in this hotel.

SARAH. They don't. I don't believe it.

MR MICHAELS. You don't believe me! Go on then, try to move it. They're fixed to the floor. Go on, push, try to move it. Push it.

The chair doesn't move.

SARAH. You're right.

MR MICHAELS. They never used to do it.

SARAH. That's really mean of them.

MR MICHAELS. They don't trust anyone, now.

CATHERINE. It is to stop all these people creeping out of hotels carrying armchairs up their jumpers.

MR MICHAELS (*loud slap*): You see. I wish I could see you in your home!

CATHERINE. I know.

Mr Michaels puts down his drink.

MR MICHAELS I've spilt it. I've spilt my drink. (*Suddenly angry.*) I've spilt it . . . do something . . . it's gone over everything.

CATHERINE (*lightly, calming him*): Come on, you don't want the whole hotel to hear about it. (*She smiles, looking at the blue liquid on the red carpet.*) Probably burn holes in the carpet, that colour. (*She looks down at him.*) Now is it safe to leave you alone with her, for a moment, while I get us some more? You're not to mention her exams. Not even a whisper. You promise me?

Mr Michaels half nods.

You're not to go on the attack as soon as my back's turned, look at me . . . (*He looks at her.*) Right.

Catherine goes.

MR MICHAELS (*sharp*): Where's she gone?

SARAH. Gone for a refill. More blue drinks.

There is an uneasy moment between them, both eyeing each other.

What are you looking at?

MR MICHAELS. What's the matter with you?

SARAH. Just a twinge of nerves about it all.

She moves up to him. Looks down into his lap.

MR MICHAELS. It's important you do well.

SARAH (*very sharp*): Remember. You *promised.*

Looks at all the wrapping paper torn up.

You have made a mess, haven't you?

MR MICHAELS (*matter of factly*): You see some sights sitting here! Women completely weighed down by jewellery, Arabs standing reading dirty magazines. Last time I was in a hotel lobby watching things go by, I suddenly saw this girl. She was well dressed, in yellow, she looked so bold, so strikking. But pale. And then my heart really jumped. Because it was Catherine. I was looking at your sister Catherine.

SARAH (*sharp*): I'd like to watch her when she didn't know I was there.

Catherine reappears, with striped yellow and pink cocktails.

MR MICHAELS (*taking the glass*): What are you trying to do to me now, kill me?

CATHERINE (*lightly*): No, just keep you quiet.

MR MICHAELS (*catching hold of her wrists*): Always wearing lots of bracelets now. She makes this clinking noise when she comes towards me. If I was going to go blind . . . I would still be able to hear you coming.

CATHERINE. But you are not going to go blind.

MR MICHAELS (*loud*): I didn't say I was. (*Catching hold of Catherine.*) Look how well dressed she is! Isn't she beautifully dressed!

SARAH (*watching her, beady-eyed*): She always is!

MR MICHAELS. Stand up, stand next to each other! I want to look at you both.

CATHERINE. Not now, Dad.

MR MICHAELS (*furiously*): Do it! Please. I see you together so seldom. (*To Sarah:*) Take the cardigan off, please take the cardigan off.

SARAH (*awkwardly*): I get bad sunburn.

She stands next to her sister.

MR MICHAELS. They are good-lookers my girls. Aren't you! (*To Catherine:*) Let's see your face properly. (*She moves.*)

And take your jacket off. (*Surprisingly forcibly.*) Go on – take it off.

CATHERINE (*lightly*): I don't think we need to give a public striptease do we.

She takes off her jacket, and stands as he gazes at her.

MR MICHAELS. I want to see you properly. You've got new shoes on, see! (*Suddenly.*) Have you still got that red bicycle, have you, that big red bicycle?

CATHERINE. That was ages ago, Dad. Ten years ago.

MR MICHAELS. You still going out with that good-looking boy Robert?

CATHERINE. That was at least eight years ago. And you know that. You haven't gone hazy again, have you!

SARAH. I go crazy when he muddles past boyfriends up. All the old ones melt together for him. Suddenly you think – 'doesn't he realise I'm not fifteen any more?'

MR MICHAELS. Do you think she's done all right? She's going to phone isn't she, before you leave me.

CATHERINE. You're breaking the rules again.

MR MICHAELS (*indicating Catherine*): She got a scholarship to a university. .

SARAH. I remember.

MR MICHAELS. You are too young to remember: I had the results framed.

CATHERINE (*lightly*): You snatched them away from me before I could see them.

MR MICHAELS (*suddenly loud*): She wrote things on her bedroom wall in French. Whole books on the wall. I didn't understand a word of what you did. Neither did your mother. You never stopped reading – books! She read like an owl. She educated herself. Whole place smelt of French cigarettes, all day long.

CATHERINE (*lightly*): You never let me finish, always screaming for cups of tea.

MR MICHAELS. You never came. I had to give you a good hiding once or twice.

CATHERINE (*slight smiles*): And I'm sure you still could.

MR MICHAELS. She owns the school she runs now, do you know that, she does . . . she owns and runs the school. They're handing it over to her — and she's opening a new one!

SARAH. I saw her there. I'm not sure . . .

CATHERINE. It's not true, Dad.

MR MICHAELS. She tells these millionaires what to do, orders them about.

SARAH. Yes, she's got an Austrian business man at the moment.

MR MICHAELS. I met her once with these seven Japanese millionaires.

CATHERINE. Swiss.

MR MICHAELS. Listen! How could I muddle up Japanese and Swiss? They were following her around like small sheep. All the way round here — I don't think there's much she can't do.

CATHERINE. Have you nearly finished, this list is getting a bit embarrassing.

SARAH (*quietly*): Yes, it is making me squirm a little.

MR MICHAELS. Her reports! You should have seen her school reports. I re-read them once a week. I used to anyway. I always knew she would go far. (*He looks at Sarah.*) Sarah, you were the normal one. You are the one that is going to get married, and settle down, and Catherine . . .

SARAH (*cutting him off*): Maybe before the night is out then, I will have got married, instead of getting the grades in my exams!

MR MICHAELS (*looking at Catherine*): She was always a great looker, but suddenly she blossomed.

SARAH. Must have been the French

cigarettes.

MR MICHAELS. And now, look at her.

CATHERINE. What are you trying to do, start a civil war between us.

MR MICHAELS (*loud, indicating Sarah*): Has she got any news for me? Has she been to phone again? I'm not leaving here till I know if she's done well or not . . .

Catherine tries to deflect him again, touches his face.

CATHERINE. Is that lipstick you've got on there.

MR MICHAELS. Don't change the subject, I want to see for myself her going to phone.

CATHERINE. It is lipstick, what have you been doing here, stalking hotel corridors, grabbing waitresses from behind!

MR MICHAELS (*loud*): Is she going to phone or not?

CATHERINE. Now come on sssh, don't start playing the tyrant . . .

MR MICHAELS. Don't sssh me. If I want to shout I will *shout*. (*He shouts this word.*) And I will go on *shouting* if I want.

CATHERINE. Have to be careful with you today, won't we?

MR MICHAELS. I have to know before you go.

SARAH. But there is no news yet, don't you understand?

MR MICHAELS. You got to go and try — they may have heard something.

SARAH. I'm not going to go — OK. There's no point Dad so just . . .

MR MICHAELS. I *want* you to. (*To Catherine:*) She's got to go and phone.

CATHERINE. Now come on, you're not to do this, you're in public.

MR MICHAELS. I want to see her go and phone. I'm not going to stop. I'm going to go on till you have. You just have to . . .

SARAH. Dad don't make such a scene, *please*. I *hate them*.

MR MICHAELS. It's not very difficult, just go over there — it may have arrived by now. I want her to phone and see.

CATHERINE. Now, sssh . . .

MR MICHAELS. Don't sssh me! I told you I'm not going to be ssshed. Are you going to phone? I want to see her.

SARAH (*loud*): Oh Dad please stop. (*She suddenly looks up and realises and backs away*.) See . . . Oh Christ — everybody is listening now.

MR MICHAELS. I don't mind who's listening, let them listen.

CATHERINE. He's not going to stop now.

MR MICHAELS (*loud*): I just want to hear, go and phone, you just have to . . .

SARAH (*furious*): All right, I will, OK.

She goes. Silence.

CATHERINE. What was all that in aid of? (*Pause. She is suddenly preoccupied — touching the furniture, moving round.*) You're being worse than usual.

MR MICHAELS (*much quieter*): I just wanted her to try. (*Pause. He is looking at her, sharp.*) What's the matter?

CATHERINE (*surprised*): With whom?

MR MICHAELS. Each meeting you start rubbing the chair — means you want to go! You look as if you need to be somewhere else.

CATHERINE. No. Of course not.

MR MICHAELS. Come here — I want to see something. (*He pulls himself out of the chair. Matter of fact.*) Just want to look at you again. I only ever get to see you for fifteen minutes. And then you disappear. You always look best in summer.

CATHERINE. Thank you.

He holds onto her arm, his manner hazy.

MR MICHAELS. I wish you'd come to

see me more often.

CATHERINE (*looks at him holding on to her, she smiles*): People might misinterpret this . . . you know.

MR MICHAELS. I want to know why you always meet me in hotels and places, and not in *your home*.

CATHERINE. I've told you, it's covered in rubbish.

MR MICHAELS. You're never untidy. (*Slight pause.*) You haven't got secrets?

CATHERINE (*smiles*): What kind of secrets?

MR MICHAELS. I expect you've got good reasons. I want news from you, of your work. I need it.

CATHERINE. Don't worry.

MR MICHAELS. I just need it so I can tell some people. It's so very difficult to *wait* for news any more.

CATHERINE. I know.

MR MICHAELS. I want you to stay longer.

CATHERINE. I can't, Dad.

MR MICHAELS. Such a busy girl, my daughter. (*Sudden shrewd look.*) You're not wasting all your ability are you?

CATHERINE. No. Come on now.

MR MICHAELS. You're going to promise me!

CATHERINE (*lightly*): What's all this now?

MR MICHAELS. Promise me.

CATHERINE (*slight pause*): OK. If you want. (*She touches him.*) I promise.

MR MICHAELS. Good. I knew it. (*Pause.*) You're a brilliant girl of course. (*He touches her.*) I like to think of you doing well. If I'd had a boy . . . if we'd had a boy — he would have been like you.

CATHERINE (*lightly*): You're pulling my hair.

MR MICHAELS. Last time I ever see you will be in a hotel foyer.

CATHERINE (*slight smiles*): On a chair nailed to the floor.

MR MICHAELS. Do you know if she's passed, tell me.

CATHERINE. Don't bully me.

MR MICHAELS. You will come and see me again soon? Before the winter.

CATHERINE. Don't be stupid, I'll see you very soon.

MR MICHAELS. You won't. You're lying. Sometimes I don't think I'll see you again.

CATHERINE. Of course you will. (*Pause.*) Don't worry. In a month or so. (*She gives a light kiss. Smiles.*) You taste of marzipan.

MR MICHAELS. She better have phoned. If she has failed, I don't . . .

Sarah enters with one small pink and blue cocktail.

SARAH. Nothing! There will be no news till this evening they said. (*Loud*:) So we can forget about it.

MR MICHAELS. She phoned did she?

SARAH (*looking at Catherine*): I bought one drink for us all to share for economy.

Sarah offers the drink to her father. He pushes it away.

CATHERINE (*to Mr Michaels*): Your insides will be like a chemist's shop window, won't they, all those colours swilling about together.

SARAH. I'm going to put him in a taxi, he's going to see his friend, Mr Conrad, and then I'll go for a walk . . .

CATHERINE. Don't worry. You can stay with me. I'll look after you. If you want.

SARAH. Can I?

CATHERINE. Of course.

SARAH. Are you sure? I know you're busy.

MR MICHAELS (*uncertainly, hazily, lost in his own world*): When is she going to hear, did you say?

SARAH. Quick, I better move him before he starts again.

Sarah downs the pink cocktail in one. Catherine drapes Sarah's cardigan round Sarah.

CATHERINE. The place we're going you'll have to look respectable.

SARAH (*smiles*): Out of school . . . away from the parent.

CATHERINE. That's right.

Blackout.

Scene Three

*The red walls of the full set − a dark
slightly faded West End red. In the back
wall a door also red but with 'Private'
on it. A few stairs of a staircase leading
off to the wings. A heavy fruit machine
standing against the back wall.*
  *Langer is standing smothered in
shopping bags, Regent and Oxford Street
carrier bags. Catherine is standing near
him. Sarah is standing staring at a large
notice in a glass case.*

SARAH (*reading*):
No jeans
No ladies trousers
No plastic containers
No alcoholic drinks not bought on the
premises
No travellers' cheques
No shorts
No dogs
No denim skirts

  She looks round.

It's a wonder anybody's allowed in here
at all. (*Pause.*) It's a wonder I am
anyway. (*She looks at Catherine.*) You
sure it's all right for me to be here?

CATHERINE. Of course it is.

LANGER. I don't think it's all opened
yet.

CATHERINE. It's just opening. Four
o'clock. There'll be a few old ladies
upstairs, where the main rooms are,
drinking lemon tea.

LANGER. Arrange for somewhere for
me to put these.

CATHERINE. I should put them down
anywhere you like − they won't get
stolen up here.

SARAH (*by the notice*): There's more:
No sandals or barefeet
(*Surprised.*) They bother to include that.
No cameras
No babies, firearms or transistor radios
No sportswear
No French bets are permitted
What are French bets? Sounds

dangerous . . . It is illegal − underlined
twice in red − and therefore absolutely
forbidden to tip the croupiers.

CATHERINE. Yes it is.

SARAH. Anyone found doing so will
lose their membership. Employees are
not permitted to fraternise with members.

  She moves from the notice.

I'll have to watch out, be careful how I
speak to the waitresses.

  *She moves excitedly across the set
  towards the window.*

CATHERINE (*to Langer, surveying the
parcels*): You look as if you have bought
most of Oxford Street. (*She smiles.*) You
must have swallowed several shops whole.

LANGER. I must thank you for making
the guards downstairs let me keep all
this with me. (*Pause.*) They knew you!

CATHERINE. Yes, I told you they
would.

LANGER (*offering money*): Here, take
it, for the tip. Go on, go on.

CATHERINE. Don't worry. Later.

  *Alan enters. He is thirty years old,
  good-looking, London accent. He has
  a bunch of keys in his hand and
  glances down looking through them
  for a second. He is upstage, on the
  bottom stair of the staircase and they
  do not notice him for a moment.*

SARAH (*standing excitedly by the
window with her back to them*): I
expected huge chandeliers and an
enormous private swimming pool and a
few painted ceilings. Actually I didn't.
I've never thought about the London
casinos before!

CATHERINE (*to Langer*): This is not
the Playboy, but it should do.

SARAH (*she moves*): It's a very big
fruit machine. (*She moves up to low
table, very animated.*) Anyway they give
you crisps here with apple sauce. I intend
to enjoy myself to a totally disgusting
degree. (*She lifts up a sandwich.*)

CATHERINE. You don't need to eat old sandwiches, Sarah. Put it down. Go on. You can have fresh ones. And for free too!

SARAH. Free! I didn't think you got anything free in London anymore.

CATHERINE (*turns to Alan*): Could we have some beef sandwiches, please.

Pause.

ALAN (*as if he's never heard of them*): Sandwiches?

CATHERINE. Yes, you still serve sandwiches don't you?

Pause. He is looking at her.

Bread sandwiches.

ALAN. If you want food, you will have to ask a waitress. (*He looks straight at Catherine.*) I am not a waiter. (*He moves sharply to go. He suddenly turns and looks straight at Langer. Sharply.*) Are you (*He stares at him.*), are you with them?

LANGER (*surprised, suddenly rendered speechless*): I . . . I . . . sorry . . . I . . . (*He looks at Catherine.*)

CATHERINE. Yes, he is with me.

ALAN (*sharp*): Right . . . (*He looks at all three.*) So this is your party is it?

CATHERINE. Yes.

ALAN (*official*): You're quite certain about that?

CATHERINE (*looking at him*): What on earth do you mean . . . Yes of course.

ALAN. Right. (*He moves slightly, then looks straight at Sarah.*) In normal circumstances, you know, she would not be allowed in here dressed like that. In fact I'm surprised they let her in at all. (*He looks at Sarah.*) It must have been a very marginal decision. (*Pause.*) Still, it's not my job to ask her to leave – so you're in luck . . .

He moves to go.

CATHERINE (*calling after him*): Excuse me.

Alan stops, he turns to face her sharply.

ALAN. You're not going to ask me about sandwiches again I hope.

Slight pause.

CATHERINE (*slight smile*): I wasn't . . . no.

ALAN (*formally*): The tables will be open very shortly, so if you just wait till then.

He goes.

Pause.

SARAH. They've got a nice relaxed style of service here. Got a way of making you feel at home.

LANGER (*turning to Catherine*): I didn't know what he was saying. (*He smiles.*) I mustn't try to do anything without you – that is obvious to me.

SARAH (*staring after Alan*): Is that man going to come back?

CATHERINE (*also staring after him*): Possibly.

LANGER (*moving, looking about him*): Beside the theatre, this is the place I wanted to go with most.

CATHERINE. You still ought to watch your prepositions, you know. Wanted to go *to* most. *To* most.

LANGER (*staring at her very carefully, repeating it obediently*): To, to . . . Later . . . later tonight I am going to break out with my English, not worry, just burst out with everything . . . with anything . . . when I am relaxed enough tonight.

CATHERINE (*smiling*): Is that a promise or a threat?

LANGER. You'll see. I can't wait till it opens. (*He moves.*) Am I allowed to use the machine before the rest opens?

He is by the fruit machine looking at her for approval. Sarah has been staring at the machine, but she moves away as Langer approaches.

SARAH. It pays out a hundred pounds as its top prize. I haven't seen that before.

CATHERINE. They have to, otherwise nobody would ever play them here.

SARAH. A hundred pounds all in 10p pieces. It must be an incredible sight. (*Excitedly*:) A great gush of them. I wish I could see it. I don't suppose it ever happens.

LANGER (*animatedly*): I don't believe it. It must be a lie. (*He puts in ten pence pieces fast and furiously, pushing the black buttons or pulling the handle depending on the machine. To Catherine, as he feeds in the money*.) You can have some . . . to play.

CATHERINE (*lightly*): No. I can use my own if I do.

LANGER (*glancing round, putting money in the machine*): Where are all the girls I expected, with their cut-off dresses, with their special costumes.

CATHERINE. You have to be patient.

He wins some money.

LANGER. A person definitely does get a kind of release in a foreign city. (*Pause. He looks at Catherine*.) Out of the class the teacher looks different too. As, of course, you're meant to. When the teacher takes you out, do you remember that from school, suddenly you notice all sorts of things about her. She looks different. Her whole appearance changes, (*He smiles*.) and I wanted to be certain she did. So when I did all that buying . . . I bought this as well. (*He suddenly takes her by the waist*.) So! Can I . . . Can I give you this?

SARAH (*craning her neck*): What's he giving you?

LANGER. It's for you. You must take it. (*He is holding out a long thin box*.) It's an obvious present, you need one very badly. (*He takes it out of its box*.) So I got you a nice watch.

CATHERINE (*gently*): Thank you. That's very kind. But you know I can't take it.

LANGER. I'm not allowed to give my teacher gifts. (*Angry*:) I'm sure other pupils give theirs . . .

CATHERINE (*smiles*): *I* don't accept presents that's all.

SARAH. I'd take it!

LANGER. Let me try it on. (*He puts it on her arm*.) Let's see if it fits you at least.

He puts it on; it has a clasp strap.

CATHERINE (*lightly*): That's rather tight — it fits like a handcuff.

LANGER. It would give me great pleasure if you would accept it. (*He watches her trying to get it off, suddenly louder, sharp*:) *Please* . . . Come on, don't be silly.

Pause.

CATHERINE (*smiling*): I'm not sure I can get it off. No . . . (*She pulls really hard*.) There. (*She hands it back*.) Thank you but *no*.

LANGER. I will keep it for you . . .

SARAH (*nervous smile*): I'm open to offers . . .

Langer turns sharply to the machine, pushes both buttons vigorously. It pays out two coins.
Alan enters.

ALAN (*staring at Langer's vast pile of shopping*): I'm afraid I have to ask you to clear that away at once please.

LANGER (*again taken by surprise*): Sorry — what do you say? (*He looks at Catherine*.) What is it?

ALAN. You have to take them down to Security.

CATHERINE (*intervening*): He wants to keep them with him and I cleared that for him downstairs.

ALAN. No. (*Over-formally*:) It contravenes the regulations. If the management saw this — there would be trouble. (*He looks Catherine full in the face*.) I shouldn't have to explain that to you — someone who's been here a number of times before should know that.

CATHERINE. Thank you.

ALAN. I'm afraid I can only ask you once . . .

CATHERINE (*looking at him, slight smile*): And then what happens . . . ? I think we get the idea now.

ALAN. Good.

CATHERINE. But I usually find when I'm here people listen if you ask to . . .

ALAN (*cutting her off*): Could you start moving them right now please?

Sarah picks up bags immediately.

Thank you. (*He begins to move. To Catherine:*) Please could you follow me. I have a message for you.

CATHERINE (*looking at him*): A message. Really . . . what sort of message?

ALAN. An important message I should think.

CATHERINE (*slight smile*): You didn't mention anything about a message when you came in . . .

ALAN. No . . . I've just remembered.

CATHERINE. And it's for me.

ALAN. Oh yes. Very definitely for you. I think it may need an answer.

CATHERINE. Sarah, you'd better take him down to the Reception desk, and watch yourself, won't you, (*She indicates the machine.*) don't spend any money. (*Suddenly sharp:*) And I mean that . . .

SARAH (*watching her closely*): Yes Catherine . . .

CATHERINE (*smiles*): And don't go near a phone either. Don't be tempted.

LANGER. I will be back immediately you understand?

CATHERINE. I understand.

Lighting change to the door marked 'Private' in the back wall. Two wall lights come on, but the afternoon lights continue.
   Alan stands against the red back wall. Catherine moves towards him and then stops.

CATHERINE (*facing him from a distance, mouths*): What?

ALAN. It's all right — you can talk normally. You don't have to mime.

His tone is familiar, jokey, intimate. He grins at her.

CATHERINE (*surprised*): How come? I thought that was never allowed.

ALAN. Nobody should bother us here.

CATHERINE. You were being extraordinarily bossy you know. Why did you force him to move his things?

ALAN. A chance to get you on your own for a moment, nobody should bother us here. This is a black spot in security just now. I hope.

CATHERINE. Why is it different today? You usually won't let me say anything to you till you're at least half a mile away from here.

ALAN. This is perfectly safe.

CATHERINE. For how long? What happens if somebody comes?

ALAN. They won't . . . I think. The place is hardly moving yet. Besides, you're roped off. Nobody ever crosses those. People have an extraordinary respect for them for some reason.

CATHERINE. Of course, if you want to take the risk, it's your job. Though naturally it was me that found it for you. But I wouldn't have thought it was worth it.

ALAN. It will be.

CATHERINE (*suddenly noticing*): There's a camera there.

Points up to top of back wall.

ALAN (*calmly*): Where?

CATHERINE. Camouflaged with red paint. It's the ugliest one I've seen for a long time.

ALAN. Don't worry, they've made a big effort to improve their security, which means it's now vastly less effective. (*He smiles, jokey*:) They needed my electrical expertise to mend the video for them. I've re-focused some of the cameras so they're all pointing at the wrong angles.

CATHERINE. They can't be that stupid.

ALAN. I assure you they can.

CATHERINE. I think we'd better stand well apart. So if any bit of you shows up, it will only be a piece of your nose or the top of your elbow, waving about in thin air.

ALAN. I won't move.

Catherine and Alan stand well apart, either side of the door, a considerable distance separating them. Alan stands very still in his black uniform. Catherine is able to move around freely, but Alan is not.

CATHERINE. You've got a new uniform on.

ALAN (*slight smile*): I was promoted last week.

CATHERINE (*warm smile*): That's why you were sounding so officious just now. Still got the old trousers with the pockets sewn up. They're beginning to crack open a little . . .

ALAN. Yeah, I don't think they're going to last much longer.

CATHERINE (*smiles, looking at his trousers*): I get fascinated by the boys' pockets when I'm by the tables. They have to sew them up themselves, and in trying to do so they scar their trousers for life.

ALAN (*slight smile*): Like mine.

CATHERINE. If somebody comes, one of those disgusting pock-marked little men that shout all the time . . .

ALAN. There's a new one — the girls call him the Eel.

CATHERINE. Yes, what are you going to tell them you're doing here?

ALAN. I'm looking over lost property. You've left something behind and I'm helping you recover it.

He opens the door marked 'Private' a little. We see just darkness beyond.

CATHERINE (*smiles*): But they won't believe that. (*Warm smile.*) You're not meant to talk to members even in the street. You're forbidden even to *blink* at me away from the tables.

ALAN. Then I won't. (*He stares at her.*) We won't touch.

CATHERINE (*smiling*): Why did you drag me here anyway?

ALAN. Nobody dragged you.

CATHERINE. Vigorously encouraged me.

ALAN. I had to see you. Where've you been all this time? I've been getting withdrawal symptoms, not seeing you.

CATHERINE (*looks at him*): So I see. I've been working.

ALAN. You haven't had to take them to discos?

CATHERINE. You sure this is safe — being here?

ALAN. Of course.

The girl immediately enters, crosses the whole width of the stage in a rush, coming down the stairs and brushing past them. She is dressed in her skin-tight costume.

GIRL (*moves across*): I'm late. Really late. And I've still got to get made up.

She goes.

ALAN. You see — what did I tell you?

CATHERINE. I see . . .

ALAN. That's the main danger actually. Floating croupiers.

CATHERINE. Makes them sound like jelly fish. That camera is very definitely pointing straight at you.

ALAN. You mustn't worry.

CATHERINE. I'm not worrying.

ALAN. She won't come back.

CATHERINE. You want a bet.

ALAN. I don't bet with you. I'll prove it to you. I'll take that off, without setting alarms off.

He stretches forward without moving, and touches the medallion round her neck. He lifts it, to get it off.

CATHERINE (*warm smile*): That hurt.

She tilts her head down and the medallion comes off. He lets it fall onto the ground.

ALAN. See.

CATHERINE. Won't people miss you any moment. You're not at your 'post'.

ALAN. I don't open the tables for another few minutes. No real West Enders in yet. Just the old ones nibbling biscuits and waiting patiently. I've been having a lot of old ladies telling me their life-stories in the afternoons recently.

CATHERINE. Don't they always?

ALAN. They usually start, 'If I told you young man that I used . . .'

CATHERINE (*warm smile*): 'Young man.' I'd have trouble recognising you.

Alan, as he says the following speech, stretches forward and slowly takes the bracelet off her wrist.

ALAN. . . . 'If I told you young man I used to be a child actress in Hollywood, with long red plaits, you wouldn't believe me would you,' or, 'young man, you won't believe this, but my family owned a fleet of flying boats, and I flew to South Africa in full evening dress and had dances in the sky.'

CATHERINE (*slight smile as he removes her bracelet*): You'll probably get fried for each time we touch.

ALAN (*smiling*): It's also about this time in the afternoon I've started getting a lot of invitations to exotic places, Italian villas, palaces in the desert, private yachts.

CATHERINE. You should go. You're always talking of travelling again.

ALAN. They quickly retract them at the end of the game.

CATHERINE. I had an invitation the other day which is unbeatable.

ALAN. Is it?

CATHERINE. A pupil of mine, a Dutch businessman, said he wanted to share his own private submarine with me.

ALAN. He probably would have given you one if you'd asked! You must get showered with invitations all the time.

He stretches forward, and begins to take her jacket off with one hand. She neither helps not stops him.

CATHERINE. And you must be over-loaded with gossip by now, that weird jumble of things you're always over-hearing.

ALAN (*pulling one of her arms free of the jacket*): Yes. I've decided it's like being a stationary taxi driver; people muttering to themselves as they play and then suddenly blurting out terrible facts about their wives.

CATHERINE. Right, you've proved you can do it. (*She moves.*) You're looking rather pale you know, Alan.

ALAN. Naturally.

CATHERINE. I forgot, you don't really get going until the night lights start energising you, you slowly get woken by electricity.

ALAN. I'm living completely at night now. Got new hours . . . so this is my only way of seeing you.

CATHERINE. Really? You mean you don't get off at half-two any more?

ALAN. No.

CATHERINE. I see. (*She moves.*) No more early morning coffees for the moment.

ALAN. With me looking over my shoulder all the time, watching the entrances.

He undoes the top button on her blouse. Catherine: warm smile.

CATHERINE. There is a strong smell of seafood from your pockets. I always wondered what was walled up in them. Probably been there for a year or more.

ALAN. Careful, they're extremely fragile . . . my stitching.

Muzak. It cuts in and out very loudly and abruptly. They move away from each other.

ALAN. They're only checking the musak, flushing out the tubes.

CATHERINE. Yes, but I feel our discovery is getting increasingly imminent.

ALAN. No. We won't be!

CATHERINE. You think we're immune, do you?

ALAN. Almost immune.

CATHERINE. Almost is not good enough. What would they do to you . . . I've always wondered that, and of course especially now you've been promoted. (*She smiles straight at him.*) I don't want to end up floating in the Thames just because you touched me while you were here.

ALAN. You flatter yourself.

CATHERINE (*slight smile*): Do I?

ALAN. Yes. No. Maybe. (*Very warmly:*) Kate. (*He moves right up to her. Button undone.*)

CATHERINE (*slight smile*): You're the only person that ever calls me that for some reason. (*Pause. Lightly, amused smile.*) I really am expecting a siren to go off each time you touch me.

ALAN (*touching her arm*): I *have* missed you, you know.

CATHERINE. So've I, you.

ALAN. Missed seeing you among the potted plants and the potted old ladies.

(*He begins to unbutton her blouse again. With warmth:*) And never knowing when you're going to turn up.

CATHERINE (*with warmth too*): I don't mind seeing you again either. (*She touches his lips.*) It's been fifteen days.

ALAN (*grins*): You keep closer count than I do.

CATHERINE. No, I just never forget anything. I had a slight suspicion you didn't intend to stop at the bracelet.

He finishes unbuttoning her blouse.

What is this slow striptease for anyway. Why you taking such an outrageous risk today?

ALAN. Why not?

CATHERINE. I'm sure there's a reason, Alan. (*Slight smile.*) You can't be that pleased to see me.

ALAN. Can't I?

CATHERINE (*begins to unbutton his shirt*): And why are you allowed to keep every button in place? (*She smiles.*) I hope their screens are misting up.

ALAN. Yes. (*He pushes open her blouse, runs his hands over her breasts.*)

CATHERINE (*slight smile*): Your cameras fucking better be pointing in the wrong direction. (*Pause.*) Of course if they aren't this will be preserved forever.

She kisses him, a sensual but very warm kiss. The bell in the wall explodes into ringing above their heads. Catherine moves away calmly.

ALAN. It's all right, it's only the two minute bell . . . summoning me.

CATHERINE (*calmly*): Really, I thought it was at least a flood warning. (*She calmly, and totally unhurriedly does up her blouse.*) Maybe you could pick up all the things you've tossed on the floor.

ALAN (*bends down*): There's still the one minute bell to go. What's the hurry?

CATHERINE. Come on now, I have with me today an Austrian businessman and

Sarah, my younger sister. It's a big day for her today. I don't think it's advisable to leave her on her own any longer.

ALAN (*slipping the bracelet back on her arm*): Guardian Angel . . .

CATHERINE (*lightly*): I think you better not stand by this bell a minute longer.

Alan goes.

Scene Four

Lighting changes, music flowing across scene change, as Alan slides the table out and into position. A Black Jack table. Alan stands behind the table in his black suit, his profile to the audience. Cards on the table, and neat piles of different coloured chips, which are also piled in polythene bags on the edge of the table, as extra supplies.

Gentle muzak is playing as Langer moves towards the table with Sarah and Catherine behind him.

LANGER. So they are opening now are they!

SARAH. I expected to see these glamorous people out of Martini ads with jewellery popping off them into their drinks.

CATHERINE. I know.

SARAH. Instead there're just a few musty people in the other room looking like they're sitting out on Southend Pier.

CATHERINE. It *is* Monday afternoon, not a good time for them. (*She looks at Alan who is standing behind the table.*) We can use this table, can we?

ALAN (*his manner very formal*): Yes — we are now open.

CATHERINE (*to Langer*): You can sit here. (*Gentle smile.*) Take a little dip here.

LANGER. Good.

Langer sits at the table on a hard upright stool. His huge bulky shape is framed by the two girls, standing either side of him.

SARAH (*indicating Alan to Catherine*): He's the one that barked at us, isn't he, the one that was really rude.

CATHERINE. They don't encourage them to be over-polite, it takes up too much time, the boys are asked to stare at you really stoney-faced, they think people will come back without being smiled at. (*She looks at Alan.*) And they usually do, isn't that right?

ALAN (*formally*): I believe so . . .

CATHERINE. He's not allowed to say much.

SARAH. What was your message? Was it all right?

CATHERINE. Yes. It was very satisfactory.

LANGER. I will play two hands, I think. I would never think of doing this (*He smiles.*) in my home town. But during my English lessons is different. (*He glances up at Catherine.*) With my companion near me, looking after me.

CATHERINE. I wasn't going anywhere.

LANGER. Good. You mustn't anyway.

ALAN. Are you ready, sir?

Langer: sharp nod. Alan does a flourishing shuffle, as Catherine watches him.

CATHERINE. They train the men and girls in this ruined hotel high up in Piccadilly Circus above the Golden Nugget, in a ballroom with broken mirrors and crumbling plaster.

Alan deals Langer two hands.

A sergeant major type shouts and screams at them all, weeding them out like at an audition, he has them stacking canvas chairs the first day . . . to improve their co-ordination. (*She looks at Alan.*) Isn't that right, young man?

ALAN. Roughly accurate madam, yes.

Langer taps the table sharply for another card, after losing on one hand, he loses on that one.

LANGER. No good!

Alan deals, four cards, two hands, face up on the table.

SARAH (*excited smile*): What's he playing?

CATHERINE. Black Jack — it's like pontoon, but the rules are different.

Catherine is speaking quietly, so as not to put Langer off, but Sarah's tone is loud.

SARAH (*loud*): Did he lose?

Langer gets another card.

LANGER. I have lost!

He puts his arm round Catherine, who is standing by the table.

Help me have a little enjoyment.

CATHERINE (*slight smile, Sarah is watching beady-eyed*): That's what they always say.

LANGER. You can join me.

CATHERINE. No. (*Pause. She smiles.*) I might have a slight play on my own in a moment.

Alan deals Langer a card, but Langer stops him.

LANGER. Come on — I insist you have a play.

CATHERINE (*slight smile*): You *can't* insist.

LANGER (*surprised at himself*): No . . . no, I ask. (*He stares at her.*) I ask you — please.

CATHERINE. That's a little more like it.

Catherine sits on the seat next to him; Sarah is standing behind them moving from side to side.

SARAH (*staring over their shoulders with fascination*): How much are those blue counters worth . . . and how much are the pink and green ones?

Catherine stretches out thirty pounds.

Thirty pounds . . . (*She stares.*) Thirty!

Alan pushes it through the slit in the centre of the table.

(*Watching the bank notes go down:*) That shoe-horn, or whatever he's using, looks like it's come from Woolworths. What number have you got?

Catherine has been dealt her cards.

CATHERINE (*quietly*): Sixteen.

Langer goes bust.

LANGER. I am not with luck.

CATHERINE (*nodding casually for another card*): *In* luck.

SARAH. You're not having another one on top of sixteen, you won't win.

Alan gives her an extra card.

You've lost?

Alan sweeps up the counters.

CATHERINE (*lightly, in charge at the table*): You can see where people have burnt holes along here in their nervousness, couldn't bear the suspense, so they stab the table with their cigarettes.

LANGER. I will be burning holes soon all over the building.

Alan deals again.

SARAH (*moving sharply from side to side*): What did you get? What did you get Catherine . . . ?

CATHERINE (*calmly*): Sarah — you're meant to be quiet; if there were more people here you wouldn't be able to make this noise.

ALAN. A certain amount of conversation can be tolerated.

CATHERINE (*formally, to Alan*): Thank you for that information.

ALAN. It's a pleasure.

Langer loses, Sarah craning her neck in fascination.

LANGER (*to Catherine*): You aren't bringing me luck; I must do something about that mustn't I? (*He smiles.*) You look almost as if you belong on that chair sitting there bending over the gaming table. I must check from now on to see if I'm doing it right.

Catherine nods for another card, to add to her two.

SARAH. What have you got? Fifteen.

Sarah has backed away from the table, unable to keep still and watch.

Have you lost?

Pause. Catherine nods for another card, has another card, she loses.

SARAH (*excitedly*): You shouldn't have had another card.

CATHERINE. Sarah, try not to get quite so involved.

SARAH. You're losing.

CATHERINE (*relaxed smile*): Usually there's a hushed clinical sort of quiet here, everybody's movements are very small, little jerks of bits of people's bodies, indicating they've just lost hundreds, a sudden twitch of the elbow. But if you wired everybody's insides, for the real noise that was going on, you'd hear this crunching, and groaning, (*To Alan:*) cries and wailing, wouldn't you, and the churning of the gut. (*She smiles.*) Like a hundred washing machines.

LANGER (*nods for another card and goes bust*): I am beginning to spill sweat anyway, it is dropping onto the table. (*He wipes his brow.*)

SARAH (*watching, excited smile*): It feels sort of strange, people losing money at *tea time*, I'll remember, if I ever walk past here in the afternoon, to look up at the window and think about it! (*Quite sharp:*) Please don't have another card Catherine, you've got seventeen, let him go bust. (*Indicating Alan.*)

Catherine has another card. Sarah backs away.

SARAH. Did you lose again? (*Loud:*) You didn't.

CATHERINE. Sarah, if you're going to get that excited, you better go and stand over there, by the potted plants . . . you'll get yourself evicted otherwise.

SARAH (*moves over into the corner, but watches from there, excitedly calling out*): You're both down to your last one.

LANGER. No, my last two, *her* last one . . . (*Langer glances at Catherine.*)

ALAN (*formal tones*): Do you want to go on, sir?

LANGER. One last time.

Alan deals the cards. Sarah, from the corner, trying to see.

SARAH. What's happened . . . what have you got . . . you got good cards?

LANGER. I will stick. (*He doesn't take another card.*)

SARAH (*shouts across*): What number have you got? It's your last money.

Catherine has another card and sticks, the bank goes bust, they both win.

LANGER. There is a moment when you know you mustn't go on, I will stop now, and watch my teacher . . . (*He smiles.*) They know best! Isn't that right?

SARAH (*excited*): Catherine you're not going to go on? (*Catherine nods for another hand. Sarah suddenly shouts.*) You've doubled your stake, you've put everything on. You're *mad*! (*Pause.*) What cards has she got? (*Sarah doesn't dare look.*) What cards?

Catherine doesn't reply; she stares at her two cards.

ALAN. More cards?

Catherine nods, she gets another card and wins, the bank goes bust.

LANGER. She has done it! She can do this too . . .

Catherine stakes all her chips on the next hand.

SARAH. Oh, no! You're not going again. *Please.* Catherine: you'll lose *everything.* (*She is jumping up and down trying to control her excitement, then even louder, her excitement mixed with vicarious enjoyment.*) Please don't. Please — I can't watch you lose it.

CATHERINE (*calmly*): Sarah, you are not allowed to make this noise. You've got to control yourself or go.

Sarah holds still for moment. Catherine gets her first card.

SARAH (*explodes*): Six! The worst card. You've got an awful card.

Catherine gets the next card.

(*Shouts.*) Fifteen — that's the worst, the worst you can get — don't — for Godsake — have another card.

Catherine takes another card and gets twenty-one.

LANGER. Twenty-one! You see. She knew what she was doing.

SARAH. I didn't expect you to . . . (*She breaks off as she sees Catherine doubling the stake again.*) Oh, no! I don't believe it. *Please* — you'll never do it twice, that's really crazy . . . (*Sarah has gone into over-drive, totally excited.*) — Stop it, please — *Don't do* that!

In her excitement, and totally oblivious of what she's doing, Sarah grabs hold of one of the polythene bags of blue chips and waves it around, the chips fly up into the air and all over the stage, and an alarm immediately sounds in the building.

Sarah looks startled and then embarrassed.

Sorry . . . I got a little carried away. (*She holds the broken bag up. Nervously jokey.*) Will I get arrested . . .?

CATHERINE. I think it would be advisable to put it back on the table, before somebody comes in and decapitates you.

Sarah puts it back, the alarm still going on.

ALAN. You are not allowed to touch those (*Indicating the bags*) under any circumstances.

SARAH. So it seems.

ALAN. But it will be all right this time.

He makes a signal towards the camera.

CATHERINE. Who are you making signals at?

ALAN. Security, miss. They will be down to check it. I will have to close this table for a moment, all disturbed tables have to be closed.

CATHERINE (*turns to Sarah*): You better take Mr Langer downstairs and book our meal for tonight. (*She flicks the chips in her hand.*) We seem to be able to have a good one now . . .

SARAH. Yes – I better get out of here, before I do something else.

LANGER. I won't be safe until you come.

Alan and Catherine are left alone for a second facing each other across the table.

ALAN (*looking down, clearing the table*): You've won a lot.

CATHERINE. Yes. (*Pause. Quiet:*) You're beginning to look a little less ghostly pale – it must be almost lighting-up time. (*She picks up her counters, and turns.*)

ALAN (*not raising his voice, looking down at the table so it doesn't seem he's talking to her*): Kate – I've got something to tell you. (*She turns.*) . . . Later.

CATHERINE. Tell me now.

ALAN. No, it'll have to be later.

CATHERINE. That's a very obvious tease. I won't want to know later.

ALAN (*straightening, looking full at her*): You will.

Pause.

CATHERINE. Do you think they can lip read?

ALAN. We'll see.

He gives her a kiss, with an abrupt movement across the table.

CATHERINE. I saw that coming I'm afraid. (*Pause, she smiles.*) That would only be possible on a Monday afternoon! (*Pause.*) You're taking a lot of risks with your job today, Alan, aren't you . . .?

Catherine goes. Lighting change.

Alan swings the table round back into the wall unit, and goes. Catherine moves across the stage back towards the window and the large fruit machine. Sarah is by the machine.

What are you doing here by yourself?

SARAH. What does it look like? (*She puts coin in machine.*) To think people really believe a machine will pay out a hundred pounds in silver. (*She puts in another coin.*)

CATHERINE (*looking down at the empty plates of sandwiches – just one sandwich left*): You seem to have eaten almost all the food in the place.

SARAH (*putting another coin in*): Yes, I've been busy. (*She turns and looks at Catherine who's holding pound notes, about a hundred.*) You've won all that!

CATHERINE (*nonchalant*): Occasionally I join in and I tend to win. It's nothing by their standards. (*She sits in the window seat.*) I haven't won enough to send us to New York for a weekend for instance.

SARAH (*looks excited*): Is that what people really do, run out of here and jump on Concorde? Have you actually seen people do that?

CATHERINE. A few.

SARAH. Really? If only we could do that, like this weekend, away from that businessman for a start, why does he keep on barking at you like that? Anyway of course, you don't have to stay here, you can do what you like can't you, wherever you like?

CATHERINE. Maybe.

SARAH. Have you ever been here at night, Catherine? (*A silence.*)

CATHERINE. At night? Once or twice.

SARAH (*turning to the machine*): The fruit in this machine is all a strange colour, blue oranges – it's a bit disturbing.

CATHERINE (*suddenly loud*): Stop putting your *own money* in that!

Sarah turns.

If you want to do that – here.

She tosses her a coin, Sarah lets it drop without picking it up.

SARAH. No, *I'm* doing it. (*She puts more money in.*) I'd forgotten about the

French cigarettes till Dad said that . . .

CATHERINE. What?

SARAH (*turns and stares at her*): You –
when I was really small. (*Pause.*) The
smoke coming out of you in elegant
puffs, and all those piles of shiny black
penguin classics, piled high, almost
shutting out the window, Balzac or
somebody I expect they were. And those
big posters of European films, one
woman in particular staring down, I don't
know who she was . . .

CATHERINE. Jeanne Moreau.

SARAH. And everything had this
sophisticated smell, it was a sort of musky
clever smell, and you lying in the
window seat, always looking so
authoritative, sort of magisterial.

CATHERINE. I used to think there.
(*Loud.*) Don't put your own money in.
Please, Sarah.

SARAH (*ignoring her, coins go in*): It was
like walking into an exotic cupboard. I
used to go in there when you were out
and snuffle around everything, and Dad
used to make his mates from Dagenham
go upstairs to stare through the door
at it, he showed it off. Even when he
left Ford's and started the shop, he still
used to show people your room,
complete strangers sometimes.

CATHERINE. Really?

SARAH. Didn't you know that? You
suddenly look very content lying there
for some reason.

CATHERINE. Do I?

SARAH. You look refreshed. (*She hits
more coins into the machine, her tone
is nervously excited rather than
aggressive.*)

CATHERINE. Calm down love.

SARAH (*ignoring this, banging the
handles*): I used to store up things you
said, clever usable things, and re-read
your letters every week. You used to
write on my letters to you, 'this is a good
letter, well constructed and amusing'

and you'd give it marks out of ten and
send it back to me!

CATHERINE (*slight smile*): That was
only once.

SARAH. I liked it though. You wrote very
funny letters.

CATHERINE. No need to remind me
about it. About any of this.

SARAH. Come on you bloody thing.

CATHERINE. You don't have to worry.

SARAH (*swings round*): I haven't seen
you for this long for ages. I mean I've
been with you for a whole afternoon!

CATHERINE. Take a good look.

SARAH. I am.

CATHERINE. Yes, I'd noticed.

SARAH. Sorry, have I been staring? I
didn't mean to.

CATHERINE. That's all right.

SARAH. I haven't got anything out of
this! You can see this machine clenching
up as I approach, looking really mean.
Needs a good shaking! (*She starts
assaulting the machine, shaking it
vigorously, then breaks away.*)

CATHERINE. Now, come on.

SARAH. You must have realised how
important this is to me, to get a high
grade, it'll count as a university degree
like you got if it's high enough. It really
must be the worst feeling in the world
waiting for results, and there's nothing
you can do to shake it off! The feeling
of dread! (*She tosses the cushions
up in the air.*)

CATHERINE. Listen, be careful. You've
already wrecked one of their tables,
disabled one of their fruit machines, now
you're beating up their cushions.

SARAH. I want to know. (*She grabs the
last sandwich.*)

CATHERINE. So you're going to gorge
yourself before morning comes, are you?
You can't get over having something for
free can you.

SARAH. I really wish I could find out.

CATHERINE. Now stop it.

SARAH. It's all right for you, we all know you can do anything. Dad's right.

CATHERINE. Is he?

SARAH. I mean I'm not jealous, not that much really, no really I'm not. I just want to try to keep up, just a little, not to be too far behind you –

CATHERINE. That's a really stupid way to think. And you mustn't.

SARAH. I feel, and I know there's some truth in it, that everything depends on this, my life and everything! I mean . . .

CATHERINE. That's plainly complete rubbish. And I know . . .

SARAH. Is it? I don't want to fail.

They face each other.

CATHERINE. You won't. Now you're not going to over-indulge are you, because of the suspense?

SARAH. Not unless I have to.

CATHERINE. No Sarah, I mean that now. You've got to promise me you won't, keep your money to yourself, promise me?

SARAH. Why of course, if you want.

CATHERINE. Right.

SARAH. . . . Oh Catherine, make it all right.

Langer enters.

LANGER (*formidable*): You must come now . . . I am waiting.

Catherine looks up, at his harsh impatient tone, but remains in the window seat.

CATHERINE. Go downstairs please. We're just ready. Don't worry, we haven't forgotten you.

LANGER (*sharp*): But I have been waiting. Please hurry. You're late. (*He goes.*)

Catherine gets up after he's gone.

CATHERINE. Come on then.

She moves towards the exit and then stops, seeing Sarah is back staring at the machine.

CATHERINE. I told you not to use your own money.

She tosses a coin across the stage, to Sarah. Sarah puts it in the machine and turns to go, the machine whirs round, they move to leave, money starts pouring out of it. The machine pays out one of its jackpots, in a spray of coins.

SARAH (*jumping up and down encouraging it, shouts*): Go on, on, on! That's right. *Go on!*

The cascade of silver coins comes pouring out, on and on. It stops.

Pause. They both look at the pile of silver.

SARAH (*staring at the machine*): It was my shaking that did it!

Fade.

ACT TWO

Scene One

*Evening lights. Mr Michaels is sitting in
his hotel foyer chair frontstage,
surrounded by potted plants. His
overcoat is folded over his knees.*

*Sarah is holding a glass, half-full of
wine, and fluttering a fistfull of bank
notes. She is in an excitable mood, the
sight of the money has electrified her.*

SARAH (*looking down at the pound
notes in her hand*): I've still got a
surprising amount left. (*She looks at
the glass.*) But I can't quite remember
how much I've drunk. (*She moves up
to Mr Michael's chair.*) You better finish
this.

MR MICHAELS (*his manner abstracted,
staring out from his chair towards some
unseen television*): You've drunk too
much, I've never seen you drink so
much before. You should wait until
there is something to celebrate.

SARAH. Come on, before you go.
Before I put you on your train – have
one more for the road. It'll stop you
mentioning things you're not allowed
to mention, like telling people to make
phone calls to find out their exam results.

*Mr Michaels has taken the drink.
She pulls it away from him.*

On second thoughts, perhaps you better
not. You've already finished three drinks
for me, it might be pushing our luck.

She pours the drink down the plant.

MR MICHAELS. You can afford to buy
all these drinks and then you just pour
them away!

SARAH. These plants must have been
used for this before! No wonder they've
got yellow leaves. Arab ladies hastily
disposing of their cocktails as their
menfolk approach. If you dug down
here you'd probably find all sorts of
illegal things buried in a hurry. (*She
smiles.*) That's why hotel plants always
look so sickly and strange. (*Sarah's
manner is volatile and excited, but not
drunk.*)

MR MICHAELS. You mustn't spend too
much tonight. (*He is staring towards
television.*)

SARAH. Don't worry – I appear to
have plenty of money. It's lasting a long
time. (*She looks down at the notes in
her hand.*)

MR MICHAELS (*staring out towards
the 'television'*): You'll need all the
money you have for the rest of the year.

SARAH (*smiling*): You notice people
on *Mondays* much more, don't you!
Because there're no crowds. So everybody stares at everybody. That's why
Monday night is the best night to go
out! (*Affectionate smiles, touches
his head.*) You would pick this hotel
foyer – because it's got a television bar.
(*She pushes his chair.*) Sheltering in
your corner, in your jungle of potted
plants.

MR MICHAELS. They're not polite here.
They're not polite to you at all.

SARAH (*excited smile*): I could spend
my whole life in hotels now. Grazing
through the foyers, living off the bowls
of free peanuts, the free potato crisps, the
free rides, the free what's-on-in-London
brochures. Surviving twenty-four hours
a day in the big hotels. I may have to . . .
if the news tonight is bad.

MR MICHAELS. I'm sure she would
have come with you to see me off if she
could have. I thought we could have had
a drink here in this bar together, but I
had time with her anyway, I had a sight
of her, longer even than usual, that's
what matters. But now you are here

and I want . . .

SARAH. You are going to try to mention it. I can see it beginning to form in your throat. You have been warned, remember.

MR MICHAELS. I expect Catherine gave you the money, that's where you got it from. She is trying to take your mind off things. She is giving you a night out in the West End. Are you going to phone for your exam results?

SARAH (*explodes, animated rather than angry*): *I told you not to!*

MR MICHAELS. Just try quickly now, you might find something out . . .

SARAH. *I warned you!* (*She lifts her book up and moves to hit him in mock rage.*) What am I doing with this book anyway? You realise I'm the only person in England who revises after the exams *are over* . . . (*She slams the book deep into the earth in the largest potted plant.*)

MR MICHAELS (*staring out to the 'television'*): Your sister always did well. She didn't have to worry. She's calm about everything she does.

SARAH. I know! I know! (*Broad smile, animated.*) She's the one who was never there when you wanted her, never went to synagogue after the age of eleven and threatened to take you to court if you made her . . . only cooked for you very very occasionally and then it was something elaborate and foreign in a pink sauce with garlic . . . and *here I am,* ludicrously loyal, sense of duty and all that, ready to see you off on your train. (*Smiles gently.*) . . . but of course *she's* the one you hanker after . . . whatever she does.

MR MICHAELS. Yes, yes!

SARAH. What are you doing? What are you fiddling about with that for?

MR MICHAELS (*suddenly loud*): I want to leave a tip! I have to leave a tip!

SARAH. Don't worry I can do that. I'm completely stuffed with money. It is pouring out of every hole. (*She smiles.*)

I seem to be able to talk to you much easier − now you only half listen, only take in half of everything I say.

MR MICHAELS. You know you must watch how your sister does everything − how she manages people . . . she can teach you a lot. She succeeds at everything she does, she's doing tremendously well, she's an important person now.

SARAH. I am watching her. I can assure you! *Every move.*

MR MICHAELS. She can teach you how to do everything really, now you're on your own. (*He looks up at her for a moment.*) Of course you might have done well. One doesn't know. It is possible. You're quite clever − not as clever as she − but not bad. You never know. Do you need money? Five shillings. I must give you your five shillings . . . I haven't done that yet.

SARAH (*laughing*): Always give me five shillings, regardless of inflation, since I was tiny. No. (*Slow:*) I've got plenty of money, see. (*She holds money up.*) We're in this casino of all places − with faded red walls and a collection of tourists and nutters. Did you hear that?

MR MICHAELS. Yes . . . yes.

SARAH. You sure you did? (*She moves him out of the chair.*) Come on then.

MR MICHAELS. Don't do anything you shouldn't when you go out.

SARAH. That rather limits my options doesn't it?

MR MICHAELS. And don't go near any more drinks or you'll start . . .

SARAH (*gently*): Come on, stop croaking out advice. You suddenly sound so old and I hate you sounding old. I don't think you're old. I'm going to put you in a taxi to the station. I'll see you soon.

He doesn't seem to hear, she follows his television gaze.

It's like having to cut you away from the television with wire-cutters.

MR MICHAELS (*vaguely*): Yes.

SARAH (*looking at him*): I HOPE I
DON'T DISAPPOINT YOU. (*Pause.*)
Anyway. Don't you *dare* phone before
I do. I might be enjoying myself. I
might be doing anything. (*Broad smile.*)
We're on our own now! (*She gives a
light kiss, quiet:*) You taste of peppermint
you know.

Blackout.

Scene Two

*The main set — with its faded red walls
and gilt, and its red carpet. The wall lights
come on in the alcoves of the set which
contain luxury goods, perfumes, etc.,
behind glass. The distant sound of dance
music. Brochures about the West End
and tourist sights lying on low coffee
tables.*

*Catherine stands holding money. She
puts a coin in the large fruit machine.*

*Langer enters, his crisp electric blue
suit, his red face.*

LANGER (*sharp, summoning her*): Come.

*Catherine looks up in surprise, Langer
stares across at her.*

Come here.

*Catherine doesn't move. Langer's
mood throughout the scene is very
volatile, he speaks very fast, with great
force.*

LANGER. I need to make a phone call
— you must help me.

CATHERINE. Call who? (*She puts
another coin in the machine.*)

LANGER. Call my wife.

CATHERINE (*lightly, moving away from
him*): I think you might manage that
on your own . . . don't you?

LANGER (*catching hold of her*): No,
you must stay . . .

CATHERINE (*slight smile*): I'm not
usually held onto when people phone
their wives . . . (*She looks down at his
hand, smiling.*) It sounds like you might
be breaking my wrist.

LANGER (*he moves away suddenly*):
I'm sorry . . . I know . . . I didn't mean
to hurt.

*The girl appears, nineteen years old,
white bare shoulders, dark hair falling
down. She is dressed in her casino
'uniform' a very short and very
revealing dress.*

(*Calling out loudly at her, clicking his*

fingers): Here! A moment! Here!

The girl is moving across the stage ignoring this.

CATHERINE (*sharp, firm*): Please.

The girl stops.

LANGER. I need some more of those small cigars. Two packets of six. Fetch me please.

GIRL (*cutting him off*): I'm not a waitress – I can't take orders I'm afraid for either food or confectionery. (*Looks at him.*) Or, in fact, for anything . . .

CATHERINE (*effortless*): Could you get them for me please. Make an exception. Just once. We would be grateful. (*She hands her money.*) Thank you.

GIRL (*looking down at the money*): Just once. (*She goes.*)

LANGER (*as soon as the girl leaves is animated*): I *told you – you must not pay for me!* Do you hear me? You have paid now for the meal, all the wine, I looked at the bill, it was an enormous amount. *I have to ask you, very strongly,* you don't spend any more money on me. You *must* let me pay, from this moment. (*He looks at her, very sharp smile.*) I plead with you.

CATHERINE. I spent it on all of us. (*She puts a coin in the machine.*) I have enough.

LANGER. I won't let you any more. (*He picks up the phone, broad smile.*) Now you must help me use the telephone.

CATHERINE (*lightly*): You could try dialling.

LANGER (*dialling the operator with sharp decisive movements*): Did you write this? (*He indicates words written on the red wall by the telephone. He reads:*) 'Marianne was left lying here.'

CATHERINE. Tourist graffiti – it's always much neater than the native sort, and they put in the punctuation.

LANGER (*running his hand over the graffiti*): All the different nationalities, writing his experiences of London. (*He looks at her.*) You must find they have large appetites for information.

CATHERINE. Some of them.

LANGER. You could give people so much false information if you wanted, couldn't you. Allowing tourists to think all the wrong things. (*He looks at her.*) Businessmen too.

CATHERINE. You mean I could subvert whole sections of Euro-industry by pumping people full of the wrong technical jargon? (*She smiles.*) You're right.

LANGER. There is no answer. (*He waves the receiver around.*) I hope you are going to make them answer. (*He looks at her.*) You know what you are . . . to me. (*He searches for the word, staring at her standing against the red wall.*) Come on, tell me – what is the word you are?

CATHERINE. Several words spring to mind.

LANGER. No. There is only one right one.

He waves the receiver and moves slightly towards her.

CATHERINE. Don't wave it around – you won't hear it when they answer.

LANGER. In two minutes we will be too late for the theatre.

CATHERINE. I know.

LANGER. I must warn you – I am going to take risks now with my English.

CATHERINE (*slight smile*): I'm going to have to be even more vigilant, aren't I . . .?

LANGER. Oh yes. (*Suddenly sharp look.*) I have been winding myself up during the evening so I can rush at it . . . have little bursts. (*He moves, the receiver tucked under his chin.*) It can be very interesting the effect of a new language on you. The feeling of . . . (*He searches for the word for a second*:) . . . lashing out in a strange city . . .

Muzak playing.

CATHERINE. That flex seems to be getting longer somehow.

He has moved across with the phone receiver still in his hand, the coil stretching out behind him more than normal.

LANGER. One is away from everything: my work, my wife, is unreachable.

CATHERINE (*smiles*): Unreachable! Don't bank on that. I had a pupil, quite a bright one, who was sacked when I was with him. They telexed his hotel.

LANGER (*smiles*): Are you hoping that will happen to me?

CATHERINE. Of course not. Why should I?

LANGER. No. (*Suddenly:*) The person living *next to us* lost his job . . . and I had to go and get our garden hose back . . . and I can tell you. I really didn't want to go. I had to make myself. No, it's true, people you know hurry past his house like there's a disease inside, they're afraid it'll spread and contaminate them, make them overnight failures. The thing they fear the most.

CATHERINE. That was one of your bursts, was it?

LANGER. Yes, my first burst. How many marks do I get?

CATHERINE. Your English seems to have improved rather astonishingly. A bit alarmingly.

LANGER. I thought you'd never notice. I told you it would when I started taking risks.

CATHERINE (*slight smile*): You'll have to be given tougher tests then won't you?

The girl enters: her very white skin, the dress that shows her body.

GIRL. Two packets. Small cigars.

CATHERINE. Thanks. Keep the change, go on.

GIRL. I can't accept tips — and you know what I think.

CATHERINE (*smiles*): Then have a cigar. I'm sure he'll let you keep one chubby cigar, please take one.

She stretches out cigar to the girl.

GIRL. I don't really want to lose my job for a small cigar. (*Pause.*) OK. Thanks. (*She takes it hurriedly, smiles.*) 'Course got no pockets to keep it anywhere. (*She goes.*)

CATHERINE (*lightly*): I'm going to have one too, if I may.

LANGER (*who has been holding out pound notes, suddenly loud, animated — really loud*): Why do you keep doing this! I have to insist now, *I insist, absolutely insist,* you don't spend any more *money* on me!

CATHERINE (*jokey smile*): I just sometimes spoil my pupils. (*She bites off the end of the cigar.*)

LANGER (*very loud*): It makes me feel *exceptionally* embarrassed. I feel like a child. The money you've been spending on me all evening! It's over a hundred pounds now! (*Loud:*) You have to stop now. (*Quieter:*) I really *do* insist you stop doing it.

CATHERINE (*gentle smile*): I don't think you can insist.

LANGER. You're not meant to do this. Will you promise me to stop. It's the one thing I ask.

CATHERINE. The *one* thing?

LANGER (*very forceful*): I won't accept one single penny more after this.

Catherine has turned, put a coin in machine — she wins a few back — she goes on putting coins in absolutely continuously.

LANGER (*slight smile*): You can *lose* money on those you know, as well as win. (*He shouts into the phone:*) Hello! I don't think your English exchanges ever answer — they're playing night games at the other end!

CATHERINE. They'll answer.

LANGER (*animated*): It's not a joke though, I have to phone my wife at a particular time and I'm about to miss it. She *needs* one phone call a day. (*Shouts, smiling into phone.*) Where are you? Answer, answer the phone . . . (*He puts the phone under his chin.*) When my wife was pregnant, no don't go away!

Catherine has moved to the other side of the stage, but he follows her, the receiver stretching out behind him across half the stage.

I found it so difficult to give her any time at all. I had so much work on my mind. (*Speedy:*) Work, work, work! It was pulling (*Searching for the word.*) . . . brambles . . . or weeds away from my mind.

CATHERINE (*turns, faces him*): So they tell me.

LANGER (*sudden smile*): Of course. You must have heard about your pupils' wives before! (*He looks at her, leaning against the wall smoking the cigar:*) To think of all the powerful men who have passed through your hands.

Surprised pause.

CATHERINE. Did you stumble on that accidentally, or did you mean it?

LANGER. They pour out all their secrets to you I expect. You hear all their fears, and . . .

CATHERINE (*sharp*): Especially if they're about to be promoted – they become very talkative then.

LANGER (*smiling, forceful*): How many confessions have you heard? I wish I could get hold of your . . . (*He snatches for the words:*) . . . memory cells and shake out all the naked details. You must know all the different smells of aftershave off by heart – able to place them country by country.

CATHERINE. Your English is starting to really leap along. I want to know how you're managing it.

LANGER (*sharp*): Don't interrupt me – I'm on a good run. (*He swings and shouts into the phone receiver at the unanswering operator:*) It would be quicker to swim with the message! (*Quieter smile.*) You know I'm playing you don't you?

CATHERINE. Are you?

LANGER. Yes, like a fisherman playing a fish into the bank. (*Pause. Firmly:*) You must now stop being the teacher. You are not allowed to be. After a certain hour you turn into something else – a companion. And then you are only that.

CATHERINE. Am I?

LANGER. Oh yes. In the prospectus – (*Starts rummaging in his pocket, with one hand, as he holds onto the receiver with the other.*) – we're promised 'certain lady teachers to accompany the client on his evenings out for informal conversation.' YOU BECOME AN ESCORT GIRL OFFICIALLY – YOU HAVE TO.

CATHERINE. You haven't got your brochure with you have you, making sure you get what you've booked for?

LANGER (*sharp*): But that's not what I have in mind anyway.

CATHERINE. And what have you got in mind?

LANGER. No, something much more interesting than that.

CATHERINE. Sounds dangerous.

Langer is up to her – the telephone coil is stretching across the whole stage, having uncoiled to its full length, stopping just two feet short of Catherine.

I see why this stretches so far, it's to enable people to play this machine, (*points to fruit machine,*) and be on the telephone at the same time! (*She smiles.*) That's clever. (*She puts another coin in the machine and it whirs round. It doesn't pay out.*)

LANGER (*lightly*): You should stop

doing that, or you will lose. (*He takes her by the arm, he is just able to reach her while still on the phone. He holds onto her.*) You know you told me a lie.

CATHERINE (*lightly*): Which one was that?

LANGER. You said you hadn't been held onto when people phoned their wives. (*Pause.*) I think you're used to it.

CATHERINE. You might just tear this sleeve, you know.

LANGER (*lightly*): I'll buy you another. (*Suddenly realises the phone has been answered.*) Hello . . . so you are there at last! That's the longest wait I've ever had on a phone. I need to phone Saltzburg 6364. (*Sideways glance – he catches Catherine by the arm.*) Don't go away, I must have you here. (*He smiles.*) I can't call collect because she is staying with my mother-in-law. (*He holds onto her. Suddenly amazed into phone:*) How much do I put in? I don't believe you. (*His voice astonished:*) I have to put in *that much*? You must have made a mistake. It's cheaper if I dial it myself – (*shouts:*) – but I do not have the code. (*Loud, boorish:*) Go on tell me it! (*He slams down the phone.*) It is incredible how much it costs. (*He is holding onto Catherine all the time he is doing this, a very tight grip as he dials briskly with the other hand.*)

Alan enters, upstage, stands checking the scene, as if on official business.

I have to give her just one call at a very particular time, that's all she needs. (*Looking towards Alan.*) I can go on phoning this phone I hope! (*He dials.*)

CATHERINE. Here – you can use these. (*She holds out palmful of coins. He is holding onto her all the time.*)

LANGER. No thank you. No more of your money. (*He catches the phone under his chin.*) Hello! Helmut. (*The pips go, he starts pushing the coins furiously into the machine – the pips continuing all the time.*) Good Lord, this phone is greedy! (*He turns, startled that*

he has run out of loose change.*) Please . . . could you give more money. I need it quickly! Please!

Catherine hands it to him.

CATHERINE (*slight smile*): Don't worry – it's here.

LANGER (*after hastily feeding more into machine*): Hullo! Helmut, *wie geht es dir? Bist du ein braver guter Junge? Gehe nicht zu spat ins Bett.*

Catherine looks at Alan as Langer holds onto her, now by the wrist, and loudly calls down phone.

Ist deine Mutter bei dir?

Whooping noise coming out of phone, as Langer becomes more agitated.

Rufe deine Mutter! Mache nicht solchen Larm. Sie nicht so schlimm! (*Sideways to Catherine:*) He is misbehaving – making these stupid noises, he won't call his mother, won't give her the telephone, and I'm running out. (*Shouts back into phone:*) *Ich telephoniere von einer telefonzella . . .* it *is* running out . . . (*Very loud:*) *GIB deine Mutter das Telefon! . . .* The squeaks are going. (*He swings round to Catherine.*) Please, help me, more change, quickly, it's going . . . she will miss her call. Give me some money!

He forces more coins into the machine, racing to get them in, in time, the pips are going loudly.

This machine must be totally bursting with coins! It will explode in a moment. (*He shouts down the phone:*) Helmut . . . (*The phone cuts out, loud whining noise.*) It's too late. Finished. They're gone . . . (*He holds the receiver up whining.*) It is such a final noise that, isn't it. They disappear at the other end like people flying off into space. (*Broad smile at Catherine.*) It's like they no longer exist anymore. (*He puts the receiver down.*) He was making very strange noises . . .

CATHERINE (*lightly*): Maybe it wasn't

your child at all. Maybe it was the wrong number.

LANGER. I should be able to recognise my own child (*Smile.*) At least I hope so – we can forget about them now! I did my best. Maybe you're right. Maybe it was a strange child. You have more to teach me.

Alan beckoning to Catherine.

CATHERINE. Why don't you go for a wash, they start having an attendant any moment now for the peak hours, and then it starts costing money. (*She is holding the rest of the change.*)

LANGER (*pushing it away*): No more. I will wash and then we will return to the tables for a little amusement before going to my hotel. (*Moves to go.*) I know something about you now. (*He goes.*)

Catherine calmly re-lights the cigar. Alan moves towards her, dance music plays in the distance.

CATHERINE (*smiles*): What on earth are you doing out here?

ALAN. Don't worry. (*He is holding a wine glass, sips from it.*) It's under control.

CATHERINE. I don't see how you expect to get away with such blatant conduct out in the open like this!

ALAN. I told you – it's reasonably safe tonight, just a few businessmen floating around with escort girls on their arms. (*He is taking his uniform jacket off, drapes it over his shoulder looking casual. Smiles.*) I am passing myself off as a normal person.

CATHERINE. Really? And you think that looks convincing, do you, with your 'Golden Wheel' casino buttons sticking out. (*She touches the buttons on his jacket.*) and your plastic bow tie. (*She pulls it out on its elastic and lets it flick back.*) And you're not allowed to drink on duty, are you, under any circumstances?

ALAN. That's right. (*Pointed.*) He seems to have reached the pinching and grabbing stage.

CATHERINE (*casual smile*): Just over-boisterous. He's quite obedient in fact. (*She finds some money lying in the crack down the side of a chair.*) Some old coins here – must have been old tips that have been hidden here – and never picked up. (*She moves back to the fruit machine.*) I'll see if they fit.

ALAN (*watching her*): You're doing more than usual on the machines tonight.

CATHERINE (*lightly, as she plays the machine*): You're crazy you know, being out here with me. What would be done to you if you were found?

ALAN. I'd probably get disembowelled and draped round the lampposts outside. (*Moving.*) Kate . . .

The American appears, tall, lanky, well dressed, in his late thirties, clean shaven, steel-rimmed glasses.

ALAN (*immediately slips into upper-class voice with his back to the man as he moves across the stage. Alan puts shades on as he speaks. Effortlessly*): There's a new club I've just found, you ought to try it, it has a kind of tropical flavour, palm trees inside, and coloured parrots and things. Everybody I know's started going there, it's amazing how these places are springing up at the moment, isn't it?

The American has stopped and is looking at Alan.

CATHERINE (*calm smile*): There is a gentleman over there who seems to be looking at you.

Alan half turns wearing his shades and looks at him.

AMERICAN. Is this the way to the small gaming room?

ALAN (*slight smile*): Sorry – I'm just a guest here. Not a member here at all. I'm new here, just passing, I . . .

CATHERINE (*interrupting him*): He's with me.

ALAN (*turning calmly to her*): You've been here before, can you tell the gentleman where the small gaming room is?

CATHERINE. It's just through there on the left, a small red room with a lot of flowers in it.

AMERICAN. Thank you. (*Staring at their odd behaviour.*) I'll find it, I think.

ALAN (*suddenly calling after him in upper-class voice, mock outrage*): No need to hurry. Very few celebrities in tonight! Mostly people who got their membership with their airline tickets!

The American goes.

CATHERINE (*lightly*): Dangerous . . . what happens if he plays at your table?

ALAN. He won't recognise me. They never recognise you with your jacket off. (*He moves towards her.*) Kate listen now . . .

CATHERINE. What *should* you be doing now, whipping all the girls into action in the changing room, bullying them behind doors marked 'Private' . . .

ALAN. Are you listening . . .?

CATHERINE. Or are they upstairs, in their tiny rest rooms, flopped out asleep in their dresses. (*She turns back to the machine to put coins in.*)

ALAN (*raises his voice*): Kate! – come here – concentrate.

CATHERINE. Careful, that was rather loud.

ALAN (*smiles gently*): I'm leaving.

Slight pause.

CATHERINE. Leaving?

ALAN. Yes. Leaving the country. Leaving this job tonight. (*Pause. He smiles.*) Leaving the country, tomorrow.

Muzak playing.

CATHERINE. I see. Don't look now but you pocket's become completely undone. It's gaping open.

ALAN. Yes. Did you hear?

CATHERINE (*sudden smile, touches his face*): Like all the other sudden

departures before them.

ALAN (*broad smile*): No this time you ought to believe me.

Sarah appears. Sees Catherine with Alan right up to her.

SARAH. What are you doing? I've been looking for you everywhere! I thought you might have gone.

CATHERINE (*to Alan, formally*): Thank you for your help. (*Moving away from him.*) But I can manage on my own now. I have what I need. (*She talks to him like a waiter.*) You can go now.

Alan moves slightly, but remains by the stairs.

SARAH. I've put Dad on his train back home – it meant so much to him, seeing you. (*Breezily:*) I think he's got it into his head he hasn't got that much longer and all that. (*Sarah opens her very large bag.*)

CATHERINE (*surprised, seeing into bag*): What have you got in there?

SARAH. Spare sandwiches. I'm collecting them because they're free here, aren't they?

CATHERINE (*amused smile*): You haven't been eating your way from plate to plate, have you – across the whole building.

SARAH. That's right. I'm storing up the fat like a hibernating animal. (*Smiles.*) So I can withstand any lean times that may lie ahead.

She tips a plate of sandwiches in its entirety into her bag.

CATHERINE. Not *all* of those Sarah?

SARAH. Don't know how secure things are going to be after this evening, do I? (*Suddenly her tone changes:*) My results don't exist for me tonight. Not even going to *try* to find out what they are. *Till morning.* (*Smiles.*) I may not need them then.

She picks up a bowl of peanuts, and swiftly puts the whole thing in her bag.

CATHERINE. Be generous and leave them the bowl, you can't eat that.

SARAH (*reluctantly replaces the bowl, minus peanuts*): How much have you got left? (*She is taking money out of her pockets. She turns suddenly and looks at Alan.*) Is it usual for waiters or croupiers or whatever they are to eavesdrop. (*Louder:*) Is it part of their training? (*She turns to Catherine.*) I'm sure he's listening you know.

CATHERINE. He's not listening. (*To Alan.*) Are you?

ALAN. No madam.

SARAH (*sharp*): We'll give you a copy of what we've been saying to keep if you like.

CATHERINE (*calmly*): He's been trying to find out the time for me. (*Pointedly to Alan:*) Checking flight times. Go and do it now. And let me have the results.

Alan goes.

SARAH (*jokily*): The flight you're giving me – is that it? To New York? (*She moves closer to Catherine.*) How much has that pupil of yours, the businessman, been trying to give you while I've been away? A few alarm clocks? He's funny. We'll be rid of him soon. (*Touching her. Looking at her admiringly, then notices.*) You've got something there on your face, a slight smudge of ink I think it is.

CATHERINE. That's very observant of you.

SARAH (*sharp*): I notice everything. One thing I do do well. (*Surprised:*) Your sleeve seems to be slightly torn – how did that happen?

Suddenly Sarah notices Catherine's hand.

(*Astonished*): Catherine . . .

CATHERINE. Yes.

SARAH. No, don't move.

She opens Catherine's hand and stares down at a fistful of red chips.

What you got all these chips for? How much are they worth? (*Worried:*) What you going to do with them?

CATHERINE (*totally in command*): Don't worry. I need to tip a few people, as usual. Just watch.

They go.

Scene Three

*Lights with heavy red shades and long
tassles hang above the roulette table,
defining the area with bright light, wall
lights glowing on the red and gilt side
wall. The Girl is standing behind the
table, her bare shoulders looking very
white under the light. Alan is standing
still and official, at the side of the
roulette table which stretches out to the
front of the stage.*

*The American is mopping his brow,
shoulders drooped having just lost. He is
wearing a red buttonhole, rather
bedraggled. The Girl is gathering in all
the chips.*

GIRL. Red 5.

AMERICAN (*very polite*): I'm quitting
for the moment. Just got to lick my
wounds. (*Looks in the wallet, nervous
smile.*) Lick my losses. Lucky I'm not
allowed to buy you a drink because I
don't think I could afford it . . .
(*Charming smile.*) Thank you very much
anyway – you've been really very
pleasant. Really.

The American moves off and goes.

ALAN. You were lucky, he was fine.
But you must be careful, you can get some
real wind-up merchants, the ones that
try to needle you.

GIRL. I know. I had my first two
yesterday.

ALAN. And keep an eye out for the
lone girls, because they can take you
by surprise. They can be really eccentric
or even vicious, start spitting things out
at you.

GIRL. I know. I watch them from here.

ALAN. They can be very interesting
characters, some of the stray girls.

*He watches Langer, Catherine and
Sarah approach the table. Langer is
holding a cocktail. The muzak is
playing in the background.*

LANGER (*To Catherine*): You must

help me. Guide my hand, translate the
rules for me.

CATHERINE (*lightly*): You can read
them perfectly well.

LANGER. You must stay close though.

*Catherine is looking down on the
table, placing her gambling chips.*

SARAH (*watchfully*): You going to do
it as well?

LANGER. I see you're going on red, is
that a good idea?

CATHERINE (*totally composed, in
command*): They have a really odd
selection of muzak in here. (*To Alan:*)
Don't you? Old film soundtracks
suddenly pipe up, *Ben Hur, Exodus.*
Very incongruous . . .

AMERICAN (*suddenly, appearing,
hurrying in*): Wait – just a moment.
I've decided to hover again here, try
to claw back some.

LANGER. You are comfortable right
here, are you?

CATHERINE (*very calm*): I'm fine.

GIRL (*in a detached monotone*): No
more bets.

*The first spin, the ball rattling round
the roulette wheel. Catherine, very
aware of Langer standing next to her.*

LANGER (*quiet*): She's going to win
again.

The ball falls into place.

GIRL. Red *16.*

*The Girl pushes their winnings
towards Catherine and the American,
Langer has lost.*

LANGER. She has won of course. (*Slight
smile.*) Soon she'll be out of my reach. If
she gets too many winnings.

AMERICAN (*his manner transformed,
very nervous as he starts winning,
picking on the Girl*): No, no, not like
that. Give them to me in smaller piles,
five at a time. Don't you know how to
do it properly?

LANGER (*lightly*): I wanted to go to the Playboy and I'm meant to get what I want. But *she* chose this one, she brought me here. (*He glances at Catherine.*) *She* must like it.

CATHERINE (*ignoring this. To Sarah as she lays out her bets*): The real weirdos will be here soon. Different sorts, security guards come here to play before going on night shifts. A few rather handsome prostitutes drift in. You can tell what time it is by who is here.

LANGER. You must point them out at once, the people worth staring at.

CATHERINE. People always want to try to spot owners of oil tankers – of famous department stores. But the really rich have gone. Don't come to London any more. Don't come to the West End. (*She feels under table.*) This place has seen grander days.

LANGER. You mean it has to make do with all the businessmen having a once in the lifetime flutter, taking medium-sized risks. (*Gently, possessively to Catherine:*) And having once in the lifetime adventures. (*Langer's manner is unashamed in front of Alan and the Girl.*)

ALAN (*sharp*): No more bets gentlemen.

GIRL. No more bets.

AMERICAN (*picking on the Girl*): Don't rush, where did they teach you to rush. You ought to go back to Gaming College. You're not busy tonight, there is no need to rush.

ALAN (*official*): No more bets now.

CATHERINE (*whispering to Sarah as the ball rattles round*): There's always that strange smell, sort of sweaty smell of anxiety.

SARAH. You're on *red* again.

CATHERINE (*quiet*): Of course.

LANGER. You may really be paying for my plane fare if I lose this time and you win.

The muzak dips away as the ball clatters into place.

GIRL. Black 17.

Pause.

LANGER. But I've been lucky this time.

The American has won a large amount, Langer has won a smaller amount. Catherine loses.

AMERICAN (*sharp to the Girl*): I *told* you not to rush.

LANGER (*looking at Catherine moving her counters*): I've always wondered how you got these. (*He touches the medallion round her neck.*) How you afforded them just teaching. Always wondered. (*Gently:*) I'm beginning to think I know.

CATHERINE (*placing counters*): You don't mean always, you haven't known me that long – so it can't be always. Your grammar's slipping.

LANGER (*sharp*): I didn't know we were still going on with the lesson. (*Looking at her.*) I wondered if they were gifts, but you don't accept gifts.

AMERICAN (*picking on the Girl*): You've got very nicotine-stained hands. You don't look after yourself I think you may be too young for this job.

LANGER (*to Catherine*): You do this in a very professional way. The way you move around the table.

CATHERINE. People try all sorts of things. You get the very superstitious who shut their eyes and move away from the table as the ball is spinning; people that like girls with certain colour hair or a particular number of buttons on their tunic.

She looks up at the pale girl.

SARAH (*watchful*): You seem to know an awful lot about it.

LANGER (*looking at the bracelets on her wrist*): If you don't win, you must let me add to your collection.

GIRL. No more bets.

SARAH (*whispers, looking at her bets*): Why don't you change from red?

The ball spins round as the queasy muzak starts. They are grouped round the table. We can see the wheel spinning. Catherine staring at it. The ball falls into place.

GIRL (*glances at Catherine*): Black 31.

Pause. The Girl begins to push a large pile of chips towards the American. Catherine has lost again.

AMERICAN (*nervously aggressive towards the Girl, his manner transformed as he wins*): I'll do it from now on. When you've got them as far as here (*He points.*) I don't want you to touch. Just keep yourself to yourself. Let me handle it, OK? You got that?

LANGER. I think I've made a little too. Let me win a couple more times, and then we'll move on to more comfortable surroundings, relaxing in my hotel.

He puts his arm round Catherine.

AMERICAN (*muttering, picking on the Girl*): I don't know where they trained you — how you were allowed through.

CATHERINE (*calm, to Langer*): You're not leaving ink stains on my shoulder I hope.

LANGER. No. (*To Sarah as Catherine places her bets:*) Look she is quite fearless isn't she, totally in control as always. I wish I had my cine-camera and could make a film . . . home movies of a beautiful girl gambling. (*Sudden, sharp look.*) You know what you are Catherine . . .?

CATHERINE. Try telling me.

LANGER. You're a tourist trap — is that the expression?

CATHERINE (*looking at the table, calmly*): That is definitely not the expression, no.

LANGER. Yes it is. Just as much as an attractive restaurant.

The Girl standing still, staring at Catherine.

GIRL. No more bets.

The wheel is spinning.

SARAH (*peering over Catherine's shoulder*): You're betting on it being an even number are you? Red.

Catherine suddenly changes her mind — moves her counters across the table.

AMERICAN. You moved! When she said no more bets. (*To Alan:*) Did you see she moved? That's not allowed, that is against the rules, this round should be disqualified or she should move it back at once.

ALAN (*who has a perfect view, pretends he didn't see*): Did she move it? I don't think so. I didn't see anything?

CATHERINE (*calmly*): Don't upset yourself. (*She moves it back.*) It doesn't matter to me at all.

Langer is sliding his hand through her hair.

The ball clatters into place.

GIRL. Black 17.

Langer wins, the American wins a very large amount, Catherine loses. She is running out of chips.

SARAH (*who has half turned away*): Was that you or not; I didn't look . . .

LANGER. I have won again. I'm winning more than I expected. I haven't phoned my wife. Nobody knows where I am. (*Quiet, gentle:*) Anything can happen.

AMERICAN (*suddenly to Alan, grunting nervously*): You realise your pockets have come undone — you should see to that or some could accuse you of cheating.

ALAN (*dryly*): I'm aware of that, sir. I will be seeing to that, and everything else, in the rest break. (*He looks at Catherine.*)

SARAH. You're out by now, aren't you? (*Quiet:*) Time to move.

CATHERINE. Don't leap to conclusions.

Catherine takes out a whole handful of red plastic chips, out of her bag, pouring them out onto the table. She is standing in the middle looking pale but confident.

SARAH (*worried*): What are you doing with all those? You aren't . . .

ALAN (*involuntarily*): But you've changed one cheque already Cath . . . (*He cuts himself off.*)

American immediately spots this.

AMERICAN. What was he saying to you? He sounded like he knew you. What's going on? . . . what did he want . . .?

Pause.

CATHERINE (*totally in command*): He was asking if we wanted some refreshments. He probably wanted an excuse to leave the room.

SARAH (*staring at the pile of red chips, worried*): But how much money is all that worth?

LANGER (*watching her place her money*): It's like sitting next to somebody driving too fast in a car, and you're not sure if they are going to hit a tree or break the speed barrier or what, but the difference is you know *you* can't get hurt. At least *I* can't get hurt. (*He stops her hand.*) Maybe you should . . .

CATHERINE. That hurts. Just very slightly.

He lets go.

Thank you.

LANGER. I had a secretary once, who was very self-willed. (*He lowers his voice.*) I got a bit mesmerised by her and did no work. (*Quiet:*) At last I had to have her dismissed. She was a clever girl like you.

SARAH (*looking up, reading the directions hanging above the table*): How much are you putting in? You must tell me. How much are each of these worth, Catherine?

LANGER (*sharp smile*): I may have to use my right and order you away from here. Order you to take me somewhere else. This is *my* last bet. (*He puts money on.*)

GIRL (*as the wheel is moving*): No more bets.

SARAH. You must stop putting it on red. It's not going to come up.

CATHERINE (*calm*): Don't worry . . .

The ball falls into its hole as the wheel goes round. Slight pause, the Girl glances at Catherine.

GIRL. *Black* 11.

Silence for a moment.

SARAH (*little voice*): How much have you lost?

LANGER. I have won again. Extraordinary.

AMERICAN (*to the Girl*): All right you can do it this time, slowly. (*She pushes his large winnings over to him.*) Carefully . . . you know you've got a mark on your shoulder, a stain. (*He suddenly leans over, starts rubbing it.*) It's gone now. There's some on your tunic. Plenty of girls want to stand where you're standing. The trouble with girls like you is you lack self esteem, d'you realise that?

SARAH. You're beginning to lose all your savings, Catherine . . . aren't you? (*Urgent:*) Why are you going on?

CATHERINE (*totally calm*): Don't worry Sarah, I never lose.

LANGER (*firmly taking her hand from the table*): You must stop playing with your own money, enough is enough. As much as I enjoy to watch it. I have to *ask* you you really must have to stop.

CATHERINE. Your grammar has really become disgraceful again.

LANGER. *If* you have to do this – you *must* do it with my money. You have to.

CATHERINE (*ignoring this*): Sarah if you're going to look that pessimistic, stand behind me. (*Calmly:*) I assure you I always win.

SARAH (*excited*): What do you mean always . . . how often have you done this before?

AMERICAN. Somebody is shaking the table . . .

SARAH. I can't believe all this money is

going – with these pieces of plastic. .
(*She picks up a counter*.) Why can't you
leave this table now?

LANGER. You must take this money
now, at once, I should never have
allowed you to spend money on me, and
then we will leave for my hotel.

AMERICAN (*looking at the Girl*): All
right. I'm ready. You can start. (*Quieter,
spikily nervous:*) Has anybody told you,
you've got a very strange complexion.
Strange colouring, like they've been
keeping you in a refrigerator. It's always
difficult to put an age on these girls.

SARAH (*peering nervous*): At least you're
on black.

CATHERINE. Sarah, will you stop
giving me these furtive looks.

The wheel is spinning round.

(*Very calmly*): I'm going to move to red.

GIRL. No more bets.

SARAH. Oh, for Christ's sake, don't let
her lose!

The ball falls into place.

GIRL. Black 20.

SARAH (*who has backed away and is not
looking*): What was that? Have you lost?

*The American has won a huge amount
– the Girl is pushing it towards him,
a mound.*

AMERICAN. Come on hurry up, didn't
anybody tell you to move faster. I
could drown in all this. Come on hurry,
faster . . .

LANGER. He's won thousands of pounds.
You're looking at over three thousand
pounds.

SARAH (*quiet, urgent*): Catherine,
you must stop losing . . .

CATHERINE (*totally calm*): Just relax,
Sarah. I *never* lose in the end. Don't
worry.

SARAH. Never! But you are losing
Catherine – all the money you've got
is going . . . (*Louder:*) You're losing it all!

LANGER (*sharp*): I'm paying for this
evening and you have to do what I want
I'm afraid. You have to take this money.
You can't play with your own any more.

CATHERINE (*calmly*): I have to ask
you to stand back from the table and
relax. I don't lose.

LANGER. I'm telling you, you have to
stop now.

GIRL. No more bets.

*Catherine is standing by herself at
the table.*

SARAH (*almost under her breath*): Red
has to come up. It has to . . . (*Under her
breath:*) Please . . . Red . . .

GIRL (*looks at Catherine*): Are you ready?

*She spins the wheel. They watch.
Silence. Ball falls into place. Girl
looks down.*

GIRL. Black 17.

Pause. Muzak playing.

SARAH. Oh Catherine what have you
done?

CATHERINE (*moving*): Don't worry –
it's all under control, I assure you. I'll
be back. I just have to cash a cheque.

ALAN (*sharp*): I think you may find
that difficult.

CATHERINE. I don't think so.

LANGER. Now come here – you have
to come to me here.

CATHERINE (*looks at Sarah*): That little
beady stare, don't worry. *You're* not
going to end up in debtor's prison. (*She
smiles.*) You got to trust me. This is
a slight wobble that's all, nothing more . . .

AMERICAN (*scooping up his winnings,
pushing them into all corners of his
suit*): It's been an amazing run for me . . .

*Alan watching Catherine go, suddenly
realises the Girl is also staring after
Catherine.*

ALAN (*sharp*): Go on clearing the table!
(*Looks towards the exit.*) I better just

have a check in the main gaming room.
There are some new girls there that need
watching.

*Alan goes briskly. Langer glances at
Sarah who is looking shaken. A
moment's pause as the American
pockets his winnings.*

AMERICAN. You have to forgive my
violent abuse, when I'm winning I get
ruder and ruder. I get just a little nervous
as you may have guessed. When there's
really a lot at stake I go insane. (*Pause.*))
And I have to take it out on something.
(*Looks straight at her.*) Somebody I
should say.

GIRL. It just flows off me. I see a lot of
nervous people.

AMERICAN (*quiet, pleasant*): Yes I
know it's nothing special for you. I'd
like to leave you something, but I know
you aren't allowed to accept it. Anyway
if you're ever in Miami . . . no I forgot,
we aren't allowed to do that either. See
you again. (*He goes.*)

*Sarah moves away from the table.
Langer follows her holding his green
cocktail. Muzak sweeps over the stage
in one loud gust then falls to a
quieter level. The Girl remains by the
table, impassively waiting.*

SARAH. How much has Catherine lost?

LANGER. A great deal, I think.

LANGER. She's in trouble. Of course
she may have a lot of money that I
don't know about.

*Langer puts coins into the fruit
machine.*

SARAH. You don't know anything about
her.

LANGER. Of course not.

SARAH. You don't.

*Langer is bent over the machine – its
light on his face. Money comes out.*

LANGER. You know I exaggerated the
badness of my English – when I realised
I had been put in too low a class, so I
could stay in her classroom.

I came for a polishing course, and I was
put in the beginners. I came into the
room the first day and saw this bright
arrogant English girl, ordering me around,
I stuttered and stammered through her
lessons so I would not be promoted away
from her.

SARAH. That was terrible of you.

LANGER. I know I have been behaving
like everybody's worst idea of the
businessman abroad. You know, the
bottom-pinching, loud and clumsy. But
there is something about her that
provokes that response. I think she
expects all her pupils to behave the same.
The way she calls them pupils – she is
there to serve but she acts the opposite
way. She hasn't even asked me what I
make. What work I do. I make components
for kitchen hardware. Middle management.
I was born in Austria, I work in Germany.

SARAH. She'll ask you.

LANGER. As it happens is an important
time in my career. I could go on
moving along up or stay still. There's a
lot of competition you understand.

SARAH. Yes.

LANGER. People forget it doesn't matter
what people look like. When you go into
a bank how do you know what the people
are thinking there? They look very
correct, very crisp. Underneath they are
as crazy as everybody else. As much as
the people with green hair and ten-inch
finger nails. More so. The same where I
work. And she hasn't seen that side of
me. (*He looks down at all the coins in
his hand and smiles. Lightly:*) I have so
much money here *I* can do crazy things
if I want. Indeed there is something I
really want to do.

*He crosses to the phone and without
lifting the receiver, forces down the
phone a whole fistful of coins, in a
vigorous assault.*

It will probably have a heart attack, with
the surprise! (*He turns, sharp self-mocking
smile.*) One of the most satisfying things
I've ever done. To be brutal, I have paid

for this evening and I am owed her company.

SARAH (*worried*): I don't know where she's gone!

LANGER. She must be trying to find a way of getting her money back. But I don't see how she can. She's taking risks, your sister, tonight. You know she could lose everything.

SARAH. She won't.

LANGER. I see. (*Gentle:*) You're so very loyal. She must be something of a hero to you. I'm sure you've never seen her like this before.

SARAH. She knows exactly what she's doing. She's talking of sending me to New York for a weekend. And if she says so, she'll manage it.

LANGER. Of course. (*He moves to go. Turns.*) SHE WILL HAVE TO COME TO ME FOR HELP. You see. I know she will.

SARAH (*having bottled it up, burst out*): Well I know certain things about her too, like how bright she is for a start! I know she doesn't usually make mistakes. She's never been in trouble in her life! If she's had a slight aberration, she'll get out of it. I know that.

Slight pause.

LANGER (*savage smile*): I'm sure you're right.

Blackout.

Scene Four

A section of the back wall containing the door marked 'Private' slides forward. The red wall in this section opens like a sliding door revealing a large box room cupboard area. A bare light bulb is hanging down inside it. The interior is unlit initially. Wall lights are on either side of the cupboard area.

Alan is standing by the entrance. Catherine enters moving across the stage towards him.

ALAN. What have you been doing?

CATHERINE (*calmly*): I've come to see you.

ALAN. You haven't tried again, have you — you haven't lost some more.

CATHERINE. No. Don't look so alarmed. You might start making me nervous.

ALAN (*slight smile*): That wouldn't be possible.

CATHERINE (*bent over the fruit machine, light on her face*): No. (*She puts coin in the machine.*) I may have to ask you for a loan. It's just possible. A small one. Merely for half-an-hour.· In order to get all this money back . . .

ALAN (*dropping his voice*): What on earth are you mentioning that out here for? (*Slight smile.*) If somebody saw me giving you money . . .

CATHERINE (*putting her last coin in*): I expect we'd manage it . . . (*She stares down at the machine, calmly*) I might just have to ask you for it though.

ALAN. You better come in here.

Alan moves her into the darkened box room, and moves in the darkness for the light switch.

CATHERINE. My first time behind the door marked 'Private'. There's a pungent aroma of something.

The light comes on; she stares around her.

Dead handbags.

A huge pile of literally hundreds of handbags, fat old leather ones, crocodile ones, gold and black ones, towers above them to the ceiling of the cupboard. In fact the pile fills almost half the box room whose walls are dusty red. Other personal belongings are mixed in with the handbags, a faded luxurious pile.

CATHERINE. Where's all this come from?

ALAN. Years of lost property, dating back to the great tourist days.

CATHERINE (*staring down at it*): Really?

ALAN. All the top quality gunge.

CATHERINE (*picking up a woman's jacket*): Ten year old fashions . . . old theatre programmes fading fast . . . (*She opens a bag.*) Old perfume . . . old shoes — I wonder how they lost them. (*She smiles.*) They must have got really excited dancing . . .

ALAN (*watching her picking away at the foot of the pile*): There was a time I'm told when people left golden bracelets or a necklace behind and didn't even bother to come back for them.

CATHERINE (*looking at the fading lost property*): Some of these people must be old women by now.

ALAN. How much have you lost Catherine?

CATHERINE (*looks round calmly*): Didn't you hear what I said — there's absolutely no need to worry.

ALAN (*lightly*): You expect me to believe that — I saw you lose.

CATHERINE. Don't worry. (*She is by wall.*)There's a crack here, did you know that? A hole — you can peer into the main gaming room. Can just see bits of people swishing past. Did you know this was here.

ALAN. Of course. One of my favourite

vantage points. (*Staring straight at her.*) For keeping an eye on things . . .

CATHERINE (*standing by the hole with her back to us. On the other side of the wall we can hear the muzak playing*): You have a whole vista of things from inside here, don't you? A voyeur's dream . . . (*She turns and looks at Alan.*) So have you got any money on you?

ALAN. Of course I haven't got any. (*Looking down at his pockets.*) You can see, there's no room.

CATHERINE (*approaching him*): What about your other pocket? (*She touches his trousers, slight smile.*) Why don't we try opening that as well. (*As she does so:*) I can smell all the different nationalities of tobacco on you tonight — blown across the tables.

ALAN (*stopping her ripping open the pockets, lightly*): That's not an especially good idea — people get rather excited when they see a torn pocket in this building. You got to forget about that now. (*He kisses her very sexually, moving his hands over her, wanting to really hold her.*)

CATHERINE (*her tone calm, detached*): Do you think there is something peculiarly stunted in our growth — that we only seem to thrive on these illicit meetings?

ALAN (*touching her*): What?

CATHERINE. Getting a particular thrill touching under 'No Exit' signs; not being allowed to speak. Then whooping down empty streets like kids when this place closes.

ALAN (*surprised by her detached tone*): It's made our work considerably more interesting for a start. (*Touching her lightly.*) Almost bearable.

CATHERINE (*touching him lightly*): Getting mild excitement out of knowing this is forbidden and almost dangerous.

ALAN. Yes. (*Lightly touching her.*) Forbidden sex . . . in ten minute instalments.

He kisses her very sexually, she responds.

CATHERINE (*then pushing him very gently away*): Like at school dances, furtive touch-ups, having a taste for a few minutes every hour against the hot water pipes, heavy petting among squashed gymn shoes.

ALAN (*staring at her*): Were you good at that?

CATHERINE. I was quite good at everything at school.

ALAN. Bet you were. What you must have been like then. Correcting all the teachers, *allowing* them to teach you, giving long rude answers in the history lessons.

CATHERINE. Certainly.

ALAN. Interrogating people after class in your school sandals at the age of eleven, with a cigarette holder.

CATHERINE. I was less obvious than that.

ALAN (*touching her all the time*): Expelling people from your secret literary society because they weren't clever enough. An alarmingly bright girl . . .

CATHERINE. We made our own elaborate rules. Totally incomprehensible except to the three of us. My friend stopped going to Mass at the age of eleven. I stopped going to synagogue at the age of ten. We broke free. Falteringly, but we did it. (*Muzak playing from behind the wall.*) We were very independent girls. Aggressively so.

ALAN. Reading and working like mad. Doing your homework as everybody else watched television.

CATHERINE. We used to lie in the long grass while the others played games, planning our futures.

ALAN. Suburban dreams . . . like I had.

CATHERINE: (*Pause.*) Our fantasies were really very explicit. Really very bold. But they were realistic too. And

we were quite determined to achieve them.

ALAN. Golden girls, weren't you? Fiercely certain of everything.

CATHERINE. That's right. Incessantly. And all the time trying to twist our North London accents into a twangy fashionable drawl.

ALAN. You knew you were capable of anything.

Pause. Catherine stares back at him.

CATHERINE. Yes. (*She turns back to the heap of belongings.*)

ALAN. *Catherine, what are you doing?*

CATHERINE (*turns*): What do you think I'm doing . . . I've lost rather a lot of money. And so I have to win it back, which I assure you I am going to do. But naturally I need some money to start with . . . (*She pulls out a hoover from the corner of the cupboard.*)

ALAN. You're not going to look in there! You won't find anything doing that.

CATHERINE. I think I will. I've seen girls do this on the back stairs . . . and this looks a very bloated hoover . . . ripe for disembowelling. It may have picked up a stray counter . . . (*She rips open the hoover with a pocket knife, a whole cloud of dust pours out.*)

I think the dust in here is a different colour – a strange casino must. (*She looks at the spilt insides.*) Some ear-rings . . . some worry beads . . . no money.

ALAN (*change of tone*): I *am* leaving you know. (*He looks at her.*) Going abroad. (*Sharper.*) Catherine . . .

CATHERINE (*stops*): I know. (*She moves up to him.*) Going on the wander again – are you?

ALAN. That's right. (*Lightly.*) I don't have your obsessive need to compete.

CATHERINE. And you mean it this time.

ALAN (*sharp*): Yes.

CATHERINE (*smiles. Lightly*): Going to try to sell your Englishness. Be hiring yourself out will you – or driving Rolls Royces in New York.

ALAN (*coming back at her*): Maybe. I hear there's a great demand for English chauffeurs.

CATHERINE. Really? (*Smiling.*) All these pale English boys driving around New York in peaked caps putting on exaggerated clipped accents, all claiming to have been to Eton . . . and it doesn't really matter if they can drive or not.

ALAN. I'll probably be checking security systems in seedy night clubs.

CATHERINE (*quiet*): Which you're good at, aren't you?

ALAN. Yes. (*Nervous smile.*) I used to make burglar alarms when I was a kid, for some weird reason. A prophetic hobby. (*His tone changes.*) It doesn't really matter what I do. I just know I have to get away. (*Pause. Pointed:*) It can't be any worse than staying here.

CATHERINE. I see. (*Pause.*) It would have been good if you could have stayed a little longer, Alan, wouldn't it? But if you have to go . . . (*She turns.*) You absolutely sure there's nothing in your pockets?

ALAN (*bewildered*): Aren't you . . . Kate . . .

She doesn't seem to hear.

(*Louder, watching her*): Even if you find something, you won't be able to use it. It will be banned from the table. (*She goes on looking.*) It is amazing you spending all this money on them . . . keeping them at arm's length by paying for everything. By having your own money.

CATHERINE. And it works.

ALAN. Buying your independence. I've even seen you insist on paying for them to go to the cloakroom – giving them the money for the tip. Remember you coming out of the Olympic in the pouring snow, looking reasonably terrific as you always do, all wound up in scarves and fur, muffled up against the cold.

CATHERINE. Leaving two very drunk Belgian businessmen alone, marooned in the casino.

ALAN (*holding her*): But underneath all these clothes, money was pouring out of you, great bundles of squashed pound notes, dropping out of your pockets, sticking out in all directions.

CATHERINE. What I'd won, yes.

ALAN. You were jam-packed with money. And so totally calm about it. So casual, totally unbothered. The two drunk businessmen must have been totally overcome.

CATHERINE (*gently*): They had an aftershave like diesel oil I remember.

ALAN. I've got a lot of pictures of you like that, stored away. Night views of you, with your businessmen. (*Holding her.*) One day all the tourist stories, all the crazy things you tell them will come home to roost. People'll come knocking at your door in the middle of the night, saying we went looking for the ancient tombs in Muswell Hill which you told us about and they weren't there.

CATHERINE. I never make things up maliciously. Only occasional flashes. (*She tries to move back to look in the heap.*)

ALAN (*stopping her, holding her*): And watching you playing the slot machines with the kids in the Las Vegas . . . in Old Compton Street. For hours and hours. And having to be almost cut away from the machines, torn from them.

Catherine turns, wanting to go on looking.

ALAN. No, stop that . . . (*Holding her.*) And you looking back over your shoulder when you leave here – like you're being pulled away from the tables against your will. (*Touching her.*) I've watched you become addicted. (*He looks at her.*) You are, aren't you, an addict?

Catherine moves, very straight and calm. Her face very pale against the red walls.

CATHERINE. I'm addicted only in the sense that I'm not going to leave here until I've got it back. And more.

ALAN. No — It's not only like that. (*Pause.*) Kate. (*Pause.*) I can tell just by looking at you now. The clothes have got a little shabbier. You're beginning to look slightly drained.

CATHERINE. Drained? Drained by what?

ALAN. From living off it, almost like you've lost a lot of blood. (*Running his hand along her lips, down her neck.*) Like needles would have done if it had been another sort of addiction.

CATHERINE. I'm surprised people don't come running up to offer me medication.

She turns away to go on looking.

ALAN (*loud*): No, don't do that. (*Sharper:*) You look older than you are Catherine. (*Quiet:*) Beginning to lose your looks. You've become the sort of person people say if you get really close to her you can see . . .

Pause.

CATHERINE. Thank you. Usually such flattery embarrasses me . . . but not tonight.

ALAN. I had to stop you ferreting around in all that junk, didn't I? (*Suddenly his tone changes, loud, trying to get her attention.*) Catherine . . . Please just give me . . . Can't you look at me. I'm going to be called back any minute! (*Louder.*) Just for a moment give me your . . . just listen to me.

CATHERINE (*calm*): I am.

ALAN (*he looks at her, then away, running his hand along the wallpaper*): Obviously . . . leaving you is not exactly easy, I mean you know how fond I am of you. (*Nervous smile.*) Probably if I use the word love, alarms will go off . . . (*He half-smiles.*) Emotion resistant alarms.

CATHERINE (*she looks around*): Not yet. (*She moves slightly.*) But some dinner-jacketed red-faced jerk will probably stick his head through that hole in the wall. (*She looks at him, quiet.*) Obviously I'll miss you too. (*She looks at him.*) Rather a lot.

ALAN. I wish you'd come with me. I know you'll say no. Come away from here.

CATHERINE. No.

ALAN (*really sharp, loud*): What on earth have you got to stay for?

Silence.

CATHERINE (*lightly*): I don't expect anybody has broken off a relationship in the broom cupboard of a casino before . . .

Muzak playing.

ALAN (*ignoring this*): I don't want to leave you here playing these games — with these men. You won't be able to stop.

CATHERINE. That's very gallant. If you got me some money it would be a help.

ALAN (*louder*): You started to think like a child would, like a child's fantasy - if you don't come up with the gold by the morning, you're going to fall captive into his hands . . .

The bell goes.

CATHERINE. Your bell. Please Alan I told you I don't want to be found with you. I am not going to be thrown out because of . . .

ALAN (*really loud*): For *Chrissake* just stop that Kate. Right. I'm not going to let you be so casual — just rush me away. I can take being made to feel I'm so lucky to know you — being *allowed* to touch you, being granted permission, I've always been able to deal with that, but I *won't* take being made to say goodbye to you like this, being allowed just a few minutes to say everything, I won't accept that. Won't let you do it. (*Very loud, near tears.*) And I don't see how you can let that happen.

Oh Christ, it would be like this, wouldn't it? Having to try to say all this with only a few minutes with the bell having gone. I just want you to . . . I don't understand you being obsessed with all this . . . Why you have to stay and . . .

CATHERINE. I told you. (*The Girl enters.*)

ALAN. I know, I'm late back. Thank you for calling me. O.K. (*She hasn't moved.*) You can go now . . .

GIRL. I think you better get there quick – because in a moment there'll be nobody on the table and they'll be grabbing everything they can . . . and we'll be responsible.

Alan looks at her and then at Catherine.

ALAN: Wait here – O.K. Don't come back in there will you? (*Looks straight at Catherine.*) I mean that.

He goes.

The Girl stands in her revealing costume, her bare shoulders looking very white. The light bulb hangs between the two girls. The pile of handbags is behind Catherine, up to the ceiling of the cupboard. The Girl continues to stare at her.

CATHERINE. He was just helping me look for something.

GIRL (*hostile*): Of course. (*Pause.*) And did he find it?

CATHERINE. No. (*Pause.*) I first met him in a cupboard as it happens. A stationery cupboard. He was hanging around the language school where I teach, looking for a job.

GIRL. Really?

CATHERINE. You haven't got any money on you by any chance?

GIRL (*looking down at her costume, skin tight across her body*): What does it

look like? (*She stares at Catherine.*) I lose my job if I talk to you.

CATHERINE. Only if someone reports you.

GIRL (*warily*): Which they will. Given half a chance.

Catherine looking very pale against the red walls, suddenly turns and breaks into violent coughing, retching, spluttering up. We cannot tell if it's a release of tension or just choking, being sick. For a moment her whole body shakes.

(*Warily*): Are you all right?

CATHERINE. Don't worry – it's only peanuts.

Pause, she turns back to face her totally composed as if nothing had happened.

I'm fine now. (*She looks around.*) Somewhere in here there must be some money. We're staring at it I know . . . (*She looks at her.*) Don't you ever get given tips?

GIRL. They aren't in money. Little tourist trophies slipped into your hand . . .

CATHERINE. You mean miniature Eiffel Towers because they have just been to Paris? That sort of thing.

GIRL. You don't get them too – do you?

Slight pause.

CATHERINE. Sometimes. They refused to cash me another cheque. I have just got to win back my money you see.

GIRL. Yes. I was watching you lose it. Half wanting to stop you. I don't usually want to stop them – you get to feel aggression here. Not just for the weirdos, and the wind-up merchants like that American just now. (*With feeling:*) Though I really do mind those. Or the really *crazy* sorts you get in the early morning. (*She stares at Catherine.*) But you start to feel that towards nearly everyone.

CATHERINE. I can imagine.

GIRL (*slight smile*): And I haven't been here long. But since the first time I've been looking at you, wondering who is that girl. Always thought you looked really confident, really arrogant sometimes – which I quite liked. The way you paid for everything for those guys, pushing money into their face.

CATHERINE. I have to escort them three nights a week. The 'school' I work for started it to keep going.

GIRL (*looking back at her*): I used to invent some really complicated stories to myself, about what you were doing here, and where you came from. (*Sharp:*) To pass the time, (*Slight pause.*) You keep on coming back here, though.

CATHERINE (*smile*): I've got kinda used to coming here, yes.

GIRL. That's already more than I've ever said to a customer here.

CATHERINE. I wouldn't want you to help me if it's going to get you into trouble.

GIRL. Who said I was going to help you?

There is a sudden ferocious banging against the back wall of the cupboard. A drunken voice yells abuse and shouting as if his mouth was directly the other side of the wall.

CATHERINE. Do they know we're in here?

GIRL. No. Just pissed. Over-excited. May start scraping at the wallpaper. Can you see him?

CATHERINE (*who has her back to us, as the shouting and banging continue*): Just flashes of pink jowls – jaws! It's such a strange feeling. All those late-night customers sliding past on the other side of that wall.

GIRL. May get his head coming through the wall any moment.

The drunken noises lessen.

CATHERINE. It's like the guys I used to have to shepherd to the motor show

when I was a courier, a guide. Suddenly went berserk.

GIRL. Yeah the things they tell you. You get to hear amazing things. Suddenly they start streaming out all those problems that are bothering them.

CATHERINE. Yes. They feel they can because they don't feel threatened by . . .

GIRL (*quietly*): By people like me you mean

CATHERINE (*stares back at her*): By us. They are so worried about success at the moment, most of them. Terrified of failure in their work. Really quite fearful. They keep on feeling the more uncertain things become, the more allergic people are to failure. They enjoy being able to tell someone about it.

GIRL. Yes. Someone to take it out on! They expect us to be really easy pickings? One of them told me I looked like the personification of soft porn. Because of the see-through uniform I suppose. I had this sensation, I felt suddenly, like I could just be poured away, just emptied, down the sink, like some suntan lotion. (*She looks at Catherine.*) He said the London girls are the easiest, like we didn't have a choice in the matter any more, like we're the bottom of the pile. There, I've told you. But luckily they aren't allowed too close to me. Because of my job.

CATHERINE. At least tourists and foreign businessmen are usually more open, more polite than . . .

GIRL (*indicating the wall*): Than yobs like that, you mean. They must all be pretty surprised at you behaving in the way you do.

CATHERINE (*slight smile*): They get surprised when I know about their subject too, can ask them questions, about the new technology in the soap industry, or the most interesting developments in video . . . You could almost do my job, they say.

GIRL. But you have to stay with them

much longer than I do. You have to deal with wandering hands and . . . You have to let them touch you, don't you. It's worse for you. (*She stares at Catherine.*) Do you have to sleep with them?

Catherine moves, trying not to show how the question hurts, then looks up, controlled.

CATHERINE. No. That I don't have to do. Not yet. What's your name?

GIRL. Mary.

Muzak behind the wall. The Girl stares at her intrigued. Silence.

GIRL. I get a pain right through me you know, having to stand for so much of the night. So, let's have a proper look, don't you think? For the money? Must be some here you can use. Let's have these down. Come on! (*She rips down a pile of handbags.*)

CATHERINE (*smiling*): They feel really cold like they belong to corpses.

They are rummaging, pulling the pile down, dust pouring.

There's nothing here.

GIRL (*really loud*): Let's go underneath! I've wanted to do this for months. (*She rips up a floorboard with no apparent effort.*) I seem to have twisted it. It won't ever fit back now! Probably find the skeletons of past unsuccessful customers in here, underneath in the dirt, they crawled in here!

The whole cupboard is filled in a swirl of dust with the girls' bodies glimpsed through a sea of flying handbags and dust. The Girl suddenly stops.

(*Really loud:*) Here! There's just one. (*She holds up a red ten pound chip.*)

CATHERINE. Great.

GIRL (*lying on her front on the floor, panting after the explosion of energy*): That really feels much better. (*She gets up to give Catherine the chip, then stops.*) I don't think I should give it to you.

CATHERINE. Why is that?

GIRL. You oughtn't to try again. Come here . . .

Catherine moves, the girl matter-of-factly rubs the dust off Catherine's face.

You manage to look good even completely covered in dust, do you know that?

CATHERINE. Maybe. (*Brushing some dust out of the Girl's hair.*) You look so young.

GIRL (*holding the chip up*): Giving you this — I'm sort of feeding something that oughtn't to be fed. Aren't I? Like giving you more and more pills. You must stop now. You may not be able to later. You ought to listen to me. (*Slight smile.*) It's one thing I do know about.

CATHERINE. Don't worry. I always manage to win. Usually.

GIRL. They all say that. I can tell you, you won't. (*Pause.*) And I mean that. (*She moves.*) I'll put you in a taxi. Come on.

CATHERINE (*firm*): No. (*She stretches out her hand.*) Can I have it? Please.

She takes it.

Blackout. They step out of the cupboard area as the muzak rises up.

Catherine emerges with the Girl. They stand still side by side as the wall moves back. Both are blinking, still covered in dust. Catherine calmly runs a comb through her hair. The Girl wipes her shoulders, wipes the dust out of her hair. Her head goes down, she shakes it violently, then looks up, pale and almost naked in her brief tunic.

The muzak rises in a great swirling movement, a great surge across the room, then dies to a barely audible level.

Alan stands behind the roulette table. Langer and Sarah are near it. The Girl crosses over and joins Alan behind the table leaving Catherine alone on the other side of the stage.

ALAN. Red 23.

SARAH. We've been scouring the building for you! I didn't know what had happened!

CATHERINE (*total control again*): Don't worry. (*She crosses up to Alan.*) I hope this table is open. (*She opens her hand.*) And this chip is admissible despite the hole through the middle of it.

LANGER (*moves forward abruptly*): No. (*His hand comes down on top of hers. His voice is firm.*) Catherine ... come here. (*He moves her determinedly away from the table.*) Come away from that.

CATHERINE. It doesn't seem I have a lot of choice, does it?

SARAH (*moving*): Can I? ...

LANGER (*firmly to Sarah*): Please stand over there. Go on, just a moment.

CATHERINE. My sister is not employed by you.

LANGER (*turning back to her*): All evening you have tried this Catherine.

CATHERINE. Tried what?

LANGER. I have booked you. I selected you. (*Slight pause.*) And so far you have eluded me ...

CATHERINE. Untrue. You've had me with you almost all the time.

LANGER. No. But I *have* had a chance to see that you are not all you seem. (*Holding her by the wrist.*)

CATHERINE. Don't be too sure about that.

LANGER. I know exactly what you're thinking about me. And I am going to have to change your mind.

CATHERINE. I can promise you that isn't possible.

LANGER. You just mean that nobody's managed it. I know you immediately likened me with other businessmen who wanted to chase you round hotel rooms, wanting their little sexual nourishment before a convention.

CATHERINE. You oughtn't to make a habit of shouting about these things in public if you want to be treated differently.

LANGER (*loud, very fast*): No, no that does not matter. (*Indicating the others.*) It's like people overhearing restaurant conversations. (*Waving towards Alan and the Girl.*) And they are just like waiters. They stare, but they can't hear, they don't listen.

CATHERINE. I can assure you one of them is.

LANGER. And I will probably not see you again in private unless I take my chance now.

CATHERINE. Please be careful, you tore my dress last time. (*She turns away.*)

LANGER (*very loud*): Catherine!

CATHERINE (*startled by this, looks at him full in the face*): Yes!

LANGER. That's better. (*He stares at her.*) That's what I wanted. I have to tell you ... I ... I ... (*Searching for the right words, quickly.*) Abroad you often see, you catch a glimpse, I'm sure everybody has done this at least once, of a girl through a train window, or stooped sorting through linen in a hotel corridor and you have a sudden totally unexpected instinct that you could share every problem you've ever had with that person, talk to her, confide in her. Share your fears. You feel certain that she will understand, even sympathise and then you move past and she is gone, and you are filled by a very big sense of loss that you didn't do it, that you missed the chance. (*Loud.*) Don't look away ... And so when I see this extremely clever girl, this very competitive girl, with a lot of contempt in her eyes ... (*Lightly:*) see her treat money like toy money. (*He pauses.*) I won't insult you with the obvious things, 'I want you as a friend, I don't

want you for . . .' (*He stops. Moves.*)
Trapped in a foreign language it is very
difficult − it sounds insincere. Everything
sounds more basic than you mean it to
be, more simple-minded, like your
tongue is made of lead suddenly. Your
mind is hundreds of feet ahead of what
you are saying and running away. (*Slight
smile.*) You can't make people understand.

CATHERINE. You seem to be doing
amazingly well. (*Lightly:*) If you will
just let me go back and complete matters
at the table.

LANGER (*his tone alters, urgent*): I
wish I could make you realise there is
my side to our meeting. I'm not just
another businessman away from his
family. However ridiculous it may seem
to you it matters to me, the intensity of
a meeting like this *with you.* And then
suddenly it goes, the sudden end. I don't
want that to . . .

CATHERINE. It would be less likely
to happen if you let me go now.

*Langer keeps grabbing hold of her,
and then letting go, only to grab her
again.*

LANGER (*slight smile*): Besides I have
time to claim. I CAN CLAIM YOU.

CATHERINE. Please.

SARAH. Catherine . . .

LANGER. I know also each time I open
my mouth you promote me into a
higher English class where, of course,
I won't be taught by you. Because my
English has become too good.

CATHERINE. That's right − you've
already gone up three classes. But you
needn't worry, it is probably my last
week anyway. My school is getting rid
of half of its teachers.

SARAH (*loud*): You're losing your job!
Must be really seedy that school, anyway.

LANGER (*really loud*): Whatever I say
Catherine, you go further away!
(*Silence.*) Slip further away. (*He moves
up to her.*) I really do know something

about you you know − there are things
I recognise. (*Touching her cheek gently.*)
Studying you as you taught me − I saw
this strange worried girl, who's not that
happy, who . . . (*He holds her head
between both his hands.*)

CATHERINE. Please . . .

LANGER. And I have to make sure you
don't vanish. (*He struggles for a second
to keep his English going − he stares
about him.*) How can I convince you?
(*A change of tone, he makes a decision.*)
I can arrange anything for you, you
know. Don't worry about the money
you've lost for a start. I can settle it.
I can pay for it all. I owe it to you. It
is because of me you have lost all your
savings. Because I was here. I can pay
for whatever you want. I will . . . I can
arrange a holiday for you abroad now
your job finishes. It's not a gift
because . . .

CATHERINE (*cutting him off*): Could
you just let me go − just for a moment.

*He lets go. She immediately moves
over to the roulette table.*

Thank you. I'm ready. Could you start
it please?

She has placed her single chip.

ALAN (*stopping the Girl*): I'm afraid
you cannot use this. I cannot let this
pass. The management would not allow
it. This is just a piece of litter.

LANGER. That is very fortunate.

CATHERINE (*to Alan calmly*): Is that
so?

ALAN (*calmly*): I'm afraid it is.

CATHERINE. OK. (*She turns and looks
straight at Sarah.*) I believe you have
some money of mine. Some of that silver
you won is mine.

SARAH. No. (*Pause.*) You're not going
to take that.

LANGER. If you just let me . . .

CATHERINE (*sharp*): Please, this is
between us. (*She turns, very firm.*)

Give me the money, Sarah.

SARAH. No. (*Steeling herself to stand up to her.*) You mustn't go on any more. You'll lose . . .

CATHERINE (*facing her*): It is necessary for me to have it Sarah. To get my money back. (*Calmly:*) You must be able to understand that.

SARAH. No. I don't. (*Pause.*) And you're not going to be able to get me to give it to you.

CATHERINE (*softening her tone*): You can have whatever you want afterwards. We'll take an early morning flight if you like, spend three days in America, or we could . . .

SARAH. You won't be able to bribe me either.

CATHERINE. I'm not bribing you. (*She stares at her, her tone soft.*) Please Sarah give me the money, I'm asking you . . . I need it.

SARAH (*watching her*): You shouldn't have got yourself into this situation. What has happened to you? I'm just not going to let you lose this as well.

CATHERINE (*suddenly very loud, almost dangerous*): You will give it to me. *Now.* Come on.

Sarah, very startled, hesitates for a moment, then gives it to her.

SARAH (*immediately after pouring a handful of silver onto table, moves away*): I shouldn't have done that. That's the stupidest thing I've ever done.

CATHERINE (*pushes silver across to the Girl*): There's ten pounds there. (*She gets a chip and immediately places it.*) Are you ready? Are you attending, you can start now. (*To Sarah, calmly:*) I'll begin by doubling it.

GIRL. No more bets.

SARAH. Giving you coins is like feeding a machine which wouldn't survive without them, isn't it?

LANGER. Please don't do this — you are probably the least wealthy person ever to have stood at the table. Your casinos will end up being used only by the croupiers and the children in the street.

SARAH. You're on red? I'm definitely not going to give you any more. Not going to feed you in instalments, do you hear?

CATHERINE. Yes.

SARAH. I won't anyway, I haven't got anything left.

The wheel spinning round.

GIRL. Red 27.

Catherine picks up her winnings, puts them back on the table.

LANGER. Now wait, just . . .

CATHERINE. Fine. I'm ready to go on at once. Thank you, you can start.

GIRL. No more bets.

SARAH. You'd better stay on red. That's right.

LANGER. Now please, I must tell you not to go any further with this now. I promise you this is not going to work out well for her.

SARAH. Why not?

The ball falls into place.

GIRL. Red 9.

SARAH. See, she's won.

LANGER. Now just . . . O.K.

Catherine puts everything she's won back on the table.

CATHERINE. I'm ready. Can you start it again please?

ALAN. We cannot move at this speed for a single customer.

CATHERINE. Can't you, you can.

ALAN. No. We have to wait to attract other people who may wish . . .

CATHERINE. Start it.

It starts.

GIRL. No more bets.

SARAH. Red, low. You've got to stay on red.

LANGER. No, please Catherine. I know, I absolutely know this will end unpleasantly.

The ball falls into place.

SARAH. How do you know? She's winning isn't she?

GIRL. Red 3.

SARAH. Yes, great, that's right.

LANGER. She's not going to be able to stop – don't you see – she is going to go on and it will be disastrous in the end. Please I'm telling you, I do know what she is trying to do, and it's not going to work out, so . . .

SARAH. Just leave her alone, she's won three times in a row hasn't she?

ALAN. The lady seems to be rushing rather excessively. (*He touches her hand.*) Why doesn't she wait a moment, and let . . .

CATHERINE. She's doing fine thank you.

GIRL. No more bets.

SARAH. Black, why? Why have you changed? You are being careful Catherine, keeping some back aren't you?

GIRL. Black 4.

SARAH. You've done it, haven't you? She's done it. Are you going again? You can't be.

LANGER. Yes she is.

SARAH. You're not are you?

CATHERINE. I just need to . . . before this runs out, the streak.

SARAH (*urgent*): Don't do that. You've got some of it back haven't you? You're not going to be completely broke. You've saved your pride. (*To Langer:*) Please don't put your hands on her anymore, O.K. (*To Catherine:*) I can't believe you're going again.

CATHERINE. Don't worry Sarah. It's going well.

LANGER. If you can't stop yourself you must use this. You must do this, use

it. Come on, don't be stupid. Please, it will be here for you anyway. Whether you win or not, it will be here.

SARAH. Can't you leave her alone for God's sake. (*She suddenly explodes:*) Just leave her! Go! It's because of you she's doing this. You can't buy her for God's sake, haven't you realised that! Just stop offering her money, like you could really buy her. Just get away from her, your time with her has run out, O.K! So just go. Wait outside or do anything, but leave her now. Go on!

Silence.

LANGER. I . . . I . . . don't understand what you say. I didn't mean to look like I was buying anything. I was just offering her the chance . . . (*He turns and goes.*)

CATHERINE (*calmly to the Girl*): Come on. I'm ready.

GIRL (*matter of fact*): Are you? (*She doesn't move.*)

SARAH (*very quiet, then she sees that Catherine has put all she has won on a single number. Astonished*): You're not putting that all on one number? You are! That's a really arrogant, contemptuous thing to do.

CATHERINE (*calmly*): Contemptuous of who?

SARAH. Of me. Of everything.

CATHERINE. Don't worry.

SARAH. Not going to watch. (*She moves away from the table, stands against the back wall.*) Probably by getting rid of him just now, I will have made your luck change, it was a mistake probably. See! Now I've started to think like you.

The Girl starts spinning the wheel.

CATHERINE. Don't call out the result, will you. I will come back and look at it. (*To Alan:*) Nor you either.

ALAN (*quiet*): Of course not.

Catherine moves away from the table as the wheel spins and joins Sarah.

CATHERINE (*slight smile, almost lightheartedly*): I don't think either of us are going to be able to go and look.

SARAH. You look so calm all the time. I don't believe you can be. How could you have done it, putting it all on one number. Why? I've got to find a way of stopping you Catherine . . .

CATHERINE. Don't worry. I can stop myself. I'm not an addict. I'm not a junkie.

SARAH. Aren't you?

GIRL. No more bets.

SARAH. I'm going to stop you somehow. Aren't you going to look then?

The ball clatters into place. Pause. She doesn't move to look.

CATHERINE. We'll just give it a moment. It might change.

Blackout.

Scene Five

Spot on Sarah using the public telephone on the wall. As she speaks she plays with some dice lying by the phone.

SARAH. Nick. No. I was just ringing for obvious reasons. Yes I know how late it is. It's nearly three o'clock in the morning — no it's just some dice I'm playing with, I'm in a sort of club, have the results gone up yet? Has anybody seen them? They have! So just tell me them then, without any preliminaries. (*Not giving the person time to reply.*) I hate it when people try to prepare you and say I've got bad news for you with that tone of sympathy in their voice, so just tell me them, then you can curl up again or whatever you were doing.

Thank you. Great. Fine. No I can't put any more coins in, the machines so full, they're sticking out of the top.

She rings off. Slight smile to herself. The whole stage lights up, as Sarah moves forward. The floor, chairs and sofa in the lounge area of the set are completely covered with money. Piles of banknotes, some in cellophane wrappings, some loose.

Catherine is lying on the sofa, smoking, surrounded by these heaps of money.

CATHERINE. Where've you been?

SARAH. Nowhere. (*Looking down at her.*) I never thought I'd be watching you lounging around in a sea of pound notes.

CATHERINE. I just had to stretch out a little. My arms have gone totally numb. It wears off.

SARAH (*picking up more money, her tone very sharp*): There's something really startling in seeing a great deal of money all in one place nowadays. More shocking than people making love in public or knifing each other — naked notes. (*She picks up money. Looks at Catherine.*) I have a strange sort of feeling that we only have a fifty-fifty chance of leaving this building with all this intact, without losing it again.

CATHERINE. No chance of us losing it. (*Suddenly sharp. She moves to the window holding notes.*) You can have some if you like, have a game or two, why don't you?

SARAH (*loud, astonished*): You mean it's still open! Oh I don't believe it Catherine. You mean there's nothing to stop you going again. You mean all this could disappear. (*Picking up armfuls of money.*)

CATHERINE. We could increase it.

SARAH. You must be the only person *ever* perverse enough to gamble and then spend the money on people who you don't like, who don't need it, and who don't want it. (*She looks at her.*) On these men.

CATHERINE (*turns*): Is he still waiting downstairs?

SARAH. I managed to send him away. You're free of him. It's funny; you nearly went broke over him, nearly wrecked yourself, and yet he was probably better than the others you've had. All you could see was the sweaty palm side of him. (*Staring at her.*) He said I must hero-worship you, which was quite sharp of him. Or maybe you think it's obvious.

CATHERINE (*picking up some money*): We could double this quite easily you know.

SARAH. Catherine, *please*, don't try it again, I'm asking you not to, it won't work this time, you'll lose it.

Alan enters, not in uniform, carrying a carrier bag.

(*Sarah hostile*): What do you want?

ALAN (*formally, like a waiter*): Is the lady feeling all right?

CATHERINE. Yes, she's fine.

ALAN (*staring at the money*): You'll manage to carry all that out between you, will you?

SARAH. Yes.

CATHERINE. I'm sure nobody's going to mind now, if you speak freely and we . . .

ALAN (*sharp, formal as if to a normal customer*): No. You must remember the rules. You wouldn't I'm sure like someone reporting you'd been fraternising too closely with a member of the staff before you had – (*He indicates the money*) – your belongings out of the building. All this could be declared null and void. Which wouldn't please you.

CATHERINE (*staring at him, quiet*): That's kind of you – to think of that.

She uses a formal tone to him from now on, but the urgency sometimes shows through.

ALAN (*looking at her, then away*): It's extraordinary the things you notice when you're leaving a place for good which you've never noticed before, like the smoke stained ceiling or the single gilt cherub with a satanic grin. (*Looking at her.*) Or what the most faithful customers look like in the morning light. (*Pause.*) Like yourself madam.

CATHERINE (*quiet*): And how do they look?

ALAN. I'll have to get used to seeing people in daylight again.

CATHERINE. You will.

ALAN. Everything will look incredibly bright. (*Nervous smile.*) I will probably suffer from migraines for the rest of my life. (*He reaches into the bag.*) I've been clearing out my locker.

CATHERINE. Like at school.

ALAN (*letting paper flutter onto the floor*): Messages from old ladies slipped into your hand as they play, it was like getting your own night mail for two years, and some photos of unsuspecting customers.

CATHERINE. Taken through a crack in the wall no doubt.

ALAN. For some reason there seems to be one of you. I thought you'd like it. (*He gives it to her.*) Well maybe I'll come across you in New York gliding down Fifth Avenue on a 24-hour visit. Suddenly there you will be in the street.

CATHERINE (*eager*): Do you have an address, I must have it. (*Then remembering:*) In case I've found I've lost something here which you might know about, and others wouldn't.

ALAN. No. I can't give you an address. I don't know where I'll end up.

CATHERINE (*really worried*): You haven't got one? (*Then formal:*) How inconvenient. (*Pause.*) If I had to find you quite quickly, in case . . . how would I . . .

ALAN (*sharp*): I don't know. Put it up in lights in Times Square.

CATHERINE. Won't your parents . . . if for some reason it was really urgent, surely I . . .

ALAN. No. They won't know. (*Pause.*) You'll find a way. (*He looks at her.*) *I* can always get in touch with *you* though, because I'll be able to find you *here* – won't I?

Sarah looks at her.

CATHERINE. Perhaps. (*Pause.*) Probably. (*Her tone quiet, concerned:*) Are you really leaving tomorrow?

Pause.

ALAN. Yes, I got to go. I have to catch the solitary night bus.

CATHERINE (*lifting some money up*): Can I? Just in case you could use it any way?

ALAN. No. Of course not. You know quite well that's forbidden.

CATHERINE. Yes, I forgot somehow . . .

Alan moves to go.

(*She calls out, still formal but urgent*): Excuse me Alan – your name is Alan isn't it – come here a moment, you've got something on your jacket. Please come here.

He comes up to her.

You've got something . . . (*She lifts her hand so that she can touch him.*) . . . in your hair. (*Calmly she moves his hair slightly and just brushes his cheek in doing so.*) You're so cold.

ALAN. Yes. (*Pause, quiet:*) Have you finished?

CATHERINE. Yes. It's gone now.

ALAN. Fine. I can go then. (*He glances down at her, formal:*) Enjoyed meeting you. Helped pass the time.

He moves to go, then turns, calls back to her.

Did you know the first night buses in the twenties used to be painted pure white. So people could seem them in the dark. These ghostly white buses crawling through the city with these green lights shining out of them. Something you told me. So I don't know if it's true or not . . . Do I? (*He goes.*)

SARAH. You must have been a good customer! Even a waiter, or a croupier, or whatever he is, gives you a personal goodbye.

CATHERINE (*quiet, preoccupied by Alan's going, staring down at the money*): I got what I lost back but I haven't made much you realise. This doesn't constitute a profit, and when it's been a lucky night you should go on, so it is said, hit a peak.

SARAH. Catherine, just don't try to prove that. It wouldn't be so bad if you actually enjoyed it. You *have* to be able to stop yourself.

CATHERINE (*quiet*): There's a fifty-five cent chance of doubling all this, red or black? (*She picks up money and moves, stops by the window.*)

SARAH. What are you doing?

CATHERINE (*her tone alters sharp – by the window:*) I saw a girl standing at the entrance to the Hyde Park Hotel the other day, in a black dress. I remember thinking she looked a little like me – rather over obviously smart, a sort of fake elegance, but quite striking, talking rather too intensely, trying to impress. I suddenly had this vision, this sense that maybe there were many of us drifting round the West End, maintaining our spirits with our little competitive fantasies. Like making this confetti money. We ought to get somebody to open this table . . .

SARAH (*suddenly loud, having to stop her*): Why can't you stop feeling that Catherine?

CATHERINE (*turns*): What?

SARAH (*loud*): Why do you feel so guilty? You're so fucking guilty aren't you. You even feel guilty about feeling guilty.

CATHERINE. Do I?

SARAH (*with passion*): Yes. Because you worked so hard to get all your qualifications and then not being able to do anything with them. Not being able to contribute anything.

CATHERINE (*quiet*): Is that right?

SARAH. However determined you were not to be reduced to just providing a cheap service and some reassurance for all these businessmen. It has really got to you, hasn't it? (*Moving around, urgent.*) Your confidence has been torn out of you, hasn't it, wrenched out, which isn't easy to conceal all the time, I know! (*Loud:*) And most of all it's about Dad isn't it, because he's weak and time's leaking away, and you so wanted to please him. (*Loud:*) Didn't you! I know you ached for that, because you're the first born and everything, and it's harder for you.

CATHERINE (*really quiet, withdrawn*): Thank you for telling me.

SARAH (*loud, shouting*): I mean I really wanted to stun him with my exam results for instance, felt everything depended on it, absolutely everything. I've passed but I haven't done that well. I haven't got the *grades* I needed. But I can't let it destroy me and I won't. (*Loud:*) I'm not going to.

Pause. Catherine with her back to her.
Did you hear any of that?

No reaction.

Look at me, come here — I want to see you properly.

CATHERINE. Sarah don't do that.

SARAH (*slight smile, close to her*): A proud animal, aren't you . . . (*Catherine tries to turn away*.) Such a proud animal. Nothing wrong in that.

CATHERINE (*very quiet, icy*): Thank you.

SARAH (*touching her*): Except you always feel you have to conquer everything completely yourself, can't turn to anybody. (*Slight smile.*) People kill themselves like that, you know.

CATHERINE (*breaks away, quiet*): I certainly don't need help.

SARAH. I knew something was happening to you, before I saw you today, hadn't seen you for months. And then I'd dreamt you'd died. My big sister was dead.

CATHERINE. Really?

SARAH. I had this weird crazy dream, you were curled up in your room, all shrivelled up, into a small skinny ball, your hair had lost all its colour — it was white . . . And you were chained to the wall. (*She smiles.*) Like the old ladies holding onto your necklace in hotel foyers. And these men . . .

Silence.

CATHERINE (*not looking at her*): Living off all this night adrenalin — as I have been doing — you skim across depression, across the surface, knowing it's there, not feeling any of it, you don't fall in and drown. (*Her tone changes, her arms wrapped round herself.*) But when it begins to wear off, and it does do, when that special kind of numbness goes, like now, then you begin to feel some sort of . . . (*She stops.*)

SARAH. You're still my clever sister, you know that, don't you?

CATHERINE (*pulling away*): And when you come down fully afterwards, it can begin to . . . you can begin to feel very small, you hardly exist, shrinking all the time, there's nothing there, nothing. Sarah I . . . No, it's all right, it's just I was so tense during the games despite all appearances to the contrary. I've bitten straight through my tongue, and it's just beginning to bleed a bit, and I . . . and just for this moment it's . . .

The wave of emotion goes through her, and she can't stop it, a real cry of pain, her body shakes, but she does not cry tears.

It does hurt a bit, Sarah. (*Louder:*) It does hurt.

Silence. It goes suddenly, she regains her composure.

It's gone. That shouldn't have happened. (*Quiet:*) I'm fine now.

SARAH. You're not. And you don't look it.

CATHERINE (*looks straight at her*): I'm all right, Sarah. Just not used to coming down like that with anybody near me. (*Quiet, slight smile.*) I've been just a little cut off from people . . .

SARAH. I know. It's only me here, though.

CATHERINE. Yes.

SARAH. Nobody else can see.

CATHERINE. You know, I do believe we've been left alone.

SARAH (*loud*): Locked up in a deserted casino.

CATHERINE. When it's quiet like this you can hear all the lifts in the old buildings in the street groaning their way up and down like they've got a life of their own. (*She looks at Sarah.*) Well you've collected enough sandwiches to last us!

SARAH (*listens for a second*): Maybe they *really* have forgotten about us, leaving us knee-deep in all this money.

In that case . . . (*She picks up dice and shakes them up.*) You're right about one thing you know, everything is luck now anyway so . . . (*She tosses up dice.*) I intend to win back half of this money. To stop you losing it. And to give me something to start off with, (*She smiles.*) in this big city.

CATHERINE. You won't manage it.

SARAH. Don't be too sure. Come on, your throw . . .

Catherine takes the dice and they start to play.

Sarah looks up, stares into the darkness, towards the back wall.

I don't think there is anyone there.

She smiles, calls defiantly into the darkness.

Don't worry, we'll let ourselves out.

Fade.

CAUGHT ON A TRAIN

Caught On A Train was first transmitted on BBC 2 on 31 October 1980, with the following cast:

FRAU MESSNER	Peggy Ashcroft
PETER	Michael Kitchen
LORRAINE	Wendy Raebeck
PRESTON	Michael Sheard
KELLNER	Ingo Mogendorf
DIETRICH	Louis Sheldon
HANS	Michael Kingsbury
SMALL MAN	John Dolan
GERMAN GUARDS	Christopher Frederick
	Ken Shaw
BELGIAN GUARD	Terry Gurry
FAT MAN	Baron Casanov
BELGIAN YOUTH	Martin Phillips
PORTER	Richard Merson
WAITER	Lex Van Delden
STEWARD	Sean Barry-Weske

Directed by Peter Duffell
Produced by Kenneth Trodd
Designed by Derek Dodd
Original music by Mike Westbrook

then back at the ticket.

PETER (*surprised at this caution*): What on earth's wrong with it?

Shot of Lorraine receding towards the train.

The ticket collector tears out part of the ticket, reluctantly gives it him back, clipping it with a short stabbing movement.

1. Exterior. Ostend Railway Station. Mid-afternoon.

A large diesel engine staring directly at the camera — the driver in a leather jacket is visible staring through the windscreen.

We pan across the front of the other platforms with the engines staring directly out towards us. One of the locomotives is roaring, ready to move.

On the soundtrack a voice is babbling fast in various languages.

We cut to the main hall of the station. Sunlight is pouring in from the big windows.

Peter is walking towards us through the bunches of people. He is twenty-seven years old, dressed immaculately in an expensive jacket and light trousers. He has dark hair, pale slightly pinched face, very sharp blue eyes. We move with him as he approaches the camera, across the concourse of the station up to the barrier.

The sound of announcements in French, then in German. They are garbled fast. In front of him is a girl, Lorraine, extremely attractive in a sleek, air hostess way. She is carrying two large suitcases. Peter watches her. The announcements change to musak. Peter is up to the ticket barrier.

The Ticket Collector is a small man with round owl-like glasses, one of which is cracked. He motions to Peter to produce his ticket, without speaking. Peter hands over a large Euro-rail ticket, the size of a booklet. The man looks at the ticket very, very carefully, almost as if inspecting for a forgery, flicking through its different sections. He glances up at Peter and gives him a piercing look through his spectacles

We move with Peter along the platform. He glances with idle curiosity towards the train on the far side with its board announcing it is going to Moscow, its engine is roaring.

Lorraine, in front of him on the platform, is struggling with her suitcases. Peter is following several paces behind, watching her.

There is a sudden noise from the far end of the platform. From Peter's point of view we see a group of kids, about seven of them, ranging from thirteen to eighteen years old, running across the railway tracks outside the station towards the platforms. They are swinging bags and shouting in German 'Wait. Wait.' They are clutching various tourist-like belongings and football scarves, suggesting they have been across to England for a football match.

One of them is blowing a loud and extremely high-pitched whistle. They jump and run across the lines as a porter shouts at them furiously in French. The noise of the engine is building to a roar. The leading boy, Dietrich, a blond boy, with a sharp pointed face, reaches the train, but remains on the track in front of it. They shout back at the porter, and realise it is the wrong train, so most of them clamber on to the platform. But two kids remain on the track in front of the train, Peter moving all the time closer to get a better look. He glances at his ticket, and moves along the side of the other train, past notices saying: 'Ostend-Bruxelles-Munich-Wien'

Dietrich rushes past him and barges into Peter as he does so.

There is no one on the train except, from one window, a small girl stares with large, blank eyes. She is eating a hot-dog. He pauses for a second and looks at her. She does not smile back.

Peter climbs aboard the train.

2. Interior. Train. Afternoon.

Peter moves through the carriage. The sun is pouring through the windows, throwing some of the carriage into deep shadow.

Peter moves through a carriage with an open gangway down the middle. The carriage is totally empty. Newspapers and magazines lie on the seats, some party hats and a half-smoked cigar on a table. On one seat lie a pair of black tights, Peter leans down and picks them up.

As he reaches the end of the carriage there is a noise behind him. Lorraine is at the other end of the carriage carrying one of her heavy suitcases and pushing the other one along in front of her, stumbling and straining, preoccupied with the effort.

Peter watches her for a second with a slight smile on his face. She is almost up to him before she notices, when she starts slightly and looks up. She stares straight at him; sharp intelligent eyes. She is dressed casually but expensively. She has long brown hair.

PETER (*a slight smile*): I was about to offer to help.

LORRAINE (*politely*): I can manage, thank you.

She moves to push past him but he takes one of the suitcases firmly away from her. He is carrying a small bag of his own.

That's very kind.

She moves through the empty train in front of him. He follows behind her carrying the enormous suitcase, truly surprised by its excessive weight. From his point of view we watch Lorraine move through the empty train. The sun is shining in, there are empty compartments wherever he looks.

PETER. It's not exactly overcrowded is it! Where is everybody?

As he moves after her, she talks without looking back at him.

LORRAINE. I'm glad to be here – little boys kept on pinching me on the boat. Coming up behind and poking me and things. (*She suddenly stops, looking back and staring at him.*) Were you on the boat?

PETER. Yes. But I wasn't one of them.

They have moved in to the couchette carriage. It is split into different compartments. Sun is still pouring through the windows. Lorraine glancing into the empty compartment as she moves.

LORRAINE. I'm in 'F'.

She stops by the compartment.

PETER. I think . . . I'm pretty sure . . . (*He puts down the case, looks at his ticket.*) We're sitting in the same compartment.

LORRAINE (*a polite smile*): Are we? That's nice. (*She moves into the compartment, looking at him.*)

PETER (*heaving the suitcase up*): Yes – we're opposite. You going far?

LORRAINE (*looking at him*): To Nuremberg. And you?

PETER. Even further.

He finishes putting the immensely heavy case on the rack.

LORRAINE (*smiles*): Thanks. (*Indicating the cases.*) I haven't got much for once – managed to travel lightly for a change. (*Her manner is totally ambiguous, impossible to tell if she is joking or not.*)

They are both standing in the compartment. Peter looks down at the tights he is still holding, and smiles charmingly.

PETER. I don't usually travel with these.

LORRAINE. Don't you?

PETER. I just found them back there.

LORRAINE (*taking the tights from him, glancing at them, matter of fact*): I wonder what they were up to this morning.

PETER (*moves back into the corridor glancing around him*): We seem to be entirely alone. (*Looking down the corridor: he smiles.*) It would be extraordinary to have a whole train completely to oneself. Fourteen carriages. Nobody else at all. (*He glances back into the compartment from the corridor.*) I take it we're on the right train? We're not going to quietly end up in Poland?

LORRAINE (*totally matter of fact*): Yes. God, it's so hot isn't it? Excuse me.

Lorraine turns away from him. She is standing in the compartment, he in the corridor. She pulls her sweater off: her blouse underneath rides up her back, showing her bare back. He watches involuntarily for a moment.

The engine of the train roars into action, whines savagely for a second and dies: both of them have looked startled.

PETER (*smiles*): Obviously only a trial run.

Lorraine joins him in the corridor. She moves up to the window: outside we can see Ostend Station, some people are milling on the platform.

LORRAINE (*staring out*): You know that feeling when you don't want other people to get on?

PETER. Yes – but I think they're going to. These are all reserved.

He flicks the metal reserved signs outside the couchette compartment,

sliding one half out then flicking it back.

LORRAINE. Perhaps they won't show up or maybe we can stop them getting in here.

PETER (*moving up to her by the window, smiling*): How?

LORRAINE. Look hostile. I'm very good at this back home. Used to think up lots of different ways of keeping people out. (*She leans out of the window, Peter watching her.*) Blow smoke at them – or you can spit at them of course. You have to really concentrate.

Peter leans out of the window beside her. A shot of Frau Messner moving with a porter across the station, talking rapidly to the porter.

PETER. I like trains. (*He is leaning out of the window.*) I haven't been on a huge train journey for years.

LORRAINE. Look.

Peter looking sideways down the train. Preston is moving along the side of the train looking determined.

PETER. I have a feeling *that one* is going to try to get on.

A sudden loud noise behind them while they watch Preston.

The door at the end of the corridor opens, and an extremely fat and large man struggles into the corridor.

LORRAINE. Come on.

They both move back speedily into their compartment and slide the door back.

Lorraine stretches herself out on the seat.

The fat man passes in the passage, his stomach brushing the glass, and moves on.

PETER. I thought he was going to puncture himself.

LORRAINE (*staring across at Peter*): It would be incredible if we really were alone.

PETER (*smiles slightly*): Wouldn't it?

Immediately their door slides open and Preston stands in the doorway. Preston is in his late thirties, but has an ageless asexual quality. He is going bald: an eggshaped head. He is wearing a huge windcheater and carrying a large all-purpose bag which he almost throws onto the luggage shelf with a sharp movement. The windcheater crackles with a grating noise every time he moves. He is wearing gym shoes. As soon as he sits he crosses his legs and does up his laces, which are already fastened, very sharply and purposefully.

(*As Preston enters, to Lorraine*): You weren't concentrating hard enough.

Preston, who is sitting by the corridor window, glances round the compartment. He notices some sweet papers over the floor, and an old newspaper – he looks straight at Peter.

PRESTON. Is this how you found the compartment? In this condition?

PETER (*surprised*): Yes.

PRESTON. You did? Fair enough.

The door slides back, Kellner enters. He too is in his thirties. He has bright red hair and heavy spectacles. He is dressed in a pin-striped suit, but a very expensive one. He carries a shiny executive suitcase – a pile of papers very carefully folded under his arm. He has a broad young face. He glances for his seat number and sits between Preston and Lorraine facing Peter.

Peter looks hard at Lorraine.

KELLNER (*as he sits, nods at Peter*): Gut. (*He places his papers – all of which are financial papers – Wallstreet Journal, Financial Times, etc. – beside him.*) Gut.

PETER (*to Lorraine, lowering his voice*): Do you think that's the lot?

LORRAINE. Maybe.

Preston glances up, his windcheater crackling.

(*Also lowering her voice*): Do you want some chocolate?

PETER (*smiles*): Chocolate? Yes . . .

LORRAINE (*she produces out of her bag a large bar of dark chocolate*): I couldn't stop myself, it was so large. (*She holds out the chocolate to Peter who takes some.*) So come on have lots.

PETER. No, just a bit.

She breaks some off and drops it into his hand: They look at each other and put the very dark chocolate into their mouths. Peter flinches as he tastes it.

LORRAINE (*looking at Peter, not raising her voice*): Christ, it's really bitter.

PETER. It's not exceptionally sweet.

LORRAINE (*leaning towards him*): You're being very English and polite.

PETER (*staring back at her*): It's revolting. (*Then lowering his voice even more.*) I think we may have got off lightly. (*Very quiet to Lorraine:*) I wonder how far they're going.

A loud noise in the passage – the sound of arguing – we hear a Porter's voice shouting in French.

Frau Messner appears in the passage, confronted by a small and excited Porter who is holding her luggage.

She stares back at him. She is in her seventies, neatly and very well dressed, but with a lot of clothes, as if it were winter. She has a strong face, a sharp abrupt and unmistakably Viennese manner. Her English is impeccable.

PORTER. Ce n'est pas assez.

He repeats this several times, holding out his hand for more, then in disgust he gives her back her small tip.

FRAU MESSNER. Aber ich habe nichts mehr!

The sound of the engine roaring again. It drowns them.

Peter turns away, his nose pressed

up against the glass – an amused smile on his face.

The engine continues roaring – but quieter. Somebody is talking to Peter in German: He does not turn round.

During the voice-over we stay on Peter.

FRAU MESSNER (*voice-over*): Entschuliegang sie haben meinen platz.

Peter turning: Frau Messner is standing right over him.

FRAU MESSNER (*polite smile*): Are you English or not?

PETER. Yes.

FRAU MESSNER. Then you can understand. You are sitting in my seat where I have to sit.

PETER. I'm sorry – this is my seat.

FRAU MESSNER. I asked for a window seat specially. I have to sit where my ticket says. (*She waves her ticket.*) You understand and I have to sit here.

PETER (*looking straight back at her, defiant smile*): But I'm afraid this is my seat – and *I* have to sit here.

FRAU MESSNER. Can I see your ticket please?

Peter glances at Lorraine then at Frau Messner. He hands over his ticket.

(*Sharp.*) You should be sitting in E.

PETER. I am sitting in E.

FRAU MESSNER. Did you ask for a window seat?

PETER. No, but . . .

FRAU MESSNER. There, I thought so. I asked for one specially. I always do.

PRESTON (*suddenly staring hard at Peter, accusingly*): Sometimes the letters get changed around.

FRAU MESSNER (*a polite steely smile*): As you see you are in my seat. (*Peter does not move.*) Do I have to say it again? I don't want to have to cause trouble.

PETER. I'm very sorry but I want to sit here and I'm going to.

FRAU MESSNER (*staring straight at him. More steely*): I don't think you understand me. I have to sit by the window. Are you going to move?

PETER. No – I am not.

Silence.

Frau Messner stares back at him in total surprise. A piercing look.

(*Defiant back.*) That is your seat – if you want to know.

He points to the seat opposite Preston.

FRAU MESSNER (*still looking at him*): Somebody must have made a mistake mustn't they? (*She moves opposite to Preston.*) I will sit here! I can never travel comfortable unless I'm by the window. Never mind – I will not call the guard.

Kellner looks very embarrassed, Lorraine looks out of the window.

PRESTON (*he leaps to Frau Messner's aid picking up her two suitcases*): Let me help you. Terrible breed porters, aren't they? Always causing trouble, the world over. It's impossible to find a helpful one. I think they have become extinct.

FRAU MESSNER. It's very kind of you. How peculiar of them to make a mistake isn't it? It has never happened before. But I won't call anybody. I will just sit here the whole journey.

A moment's silence. The sound of train doors banging.

Peter not looking at her.

Preston stares at him again.

Frau Messner is rustling about in her hand luggage: a very loud rustle.

How stupid! How very stupid of me . . . I seem to have forgotten my magazines. (*She looks at the whole of the compartment.*) I usually have a big pile of magazines to read and in the rush I have forgotten them. (*She suddenly leans over and looks at Peter.*) You don't think you could be so kind and get them for me?

A look of disbelief on Peter's face.

(*Totally unabashed.*) You just have to go over to the big bookstall and get them for me. (*The sound of train doors slamming in the distance.*) It would be a great help to me, my legs, you see, are not very strong.

PETER (*disbelieving smile*): But the train is about to go!

The sound of more train doors banging.

FRAU MESSNER. No, no, it's not. Not for ten minutes.

PRESTON. Not for thirteen minutes, to be precise. They're never off on time.

Peter gives Preston a savage look.

FRAU MESSNER. Of course you won't miss the train – it'll take you one minute. You won't even have to run.

PETER. But . . .

A whistle blows loudly – Peter looks round automatically.

PRESTON. That isn't us.

FRAU MESSNER. I have a list. (*She produces it.*) I always give them a list at the shop. (*Polite smile.*) I just have to have something to read you see.

Peter looks up. Lorraine is looking out of the window. Kellner is staring at him, as is Preston: straight at him.

A distant but urgent train announcement in the background.

Nobody says anything.

PETER. Give me the list . . .

FRAU MESSNER. That's so kind of you. I must give you money too of course. Here – there we are. (*She places the money in his hand, as she does it she looks at him.*) It is a great help to me.

PETER. You are absolutely sure I've got time.

PRESTON. You've got all the time in the world.

PETER. Because there isn't another train for a day and a half.

FRAU MESSNER. You can't possibly miss it – if you go *now*. (*Peter moves out of the compartment and slides the door shut. She looks up as he does so.*) We won't let the train go without you.

3. Exterior. Station. Afternoon.

Peter moves briskly, rather than runs down the side of the train. He glances back. A receding shot of a couple of passengers leaning out of the train window watching him go.

Peter passes the ticket collector with cracked glasses who watches him pass in surprise.

PETER (*smiling as he passes*): I'll only be a moment.

Cut to Peter standing in a queue at a news-stand. The person at the front of the queue is talking and gesticulating.

Over the loud-speakers Peter can hear trains being called. He glances up very impatiently. The sound of whistles. A loudspeaker above his head suddenly blares out brass band music.

We pan over the magazines on the news-stand, glossy Euro-magazines, Stein, Paris-Match, the Italian magazines: a mixture of terrorists and bare-breasted girls polishing cars.

Peter gets to the front of the queue and hands the man behind the counter the list. He languidly begins to collect the magazines.

We keep very close on Peter, he turns his head urgently to his right, leaning against the wall quite close to him, a

*policeman in dark glasses is staring
at him suspiciously.*

*The sound of a whistle blowing very
shrilly again and again, and an
announcement booms over a
loudspeaker, totally inaudible except
for the word 'Depart' but sounding
very urgent.*

*He glances at his watch, it says
six o'clock. He glances up at a clock
on the wall of the news-stand. It
says seven-thirty.*

*The man behind the counter comes
back with a very thick pile of
magazines. Peter pushes Frau
Messner's money into his hand. The
sound of doors slamming. The man
behind the counter looks down at
the money.*

MAN (*muttering crossly*): Ce n'est pas
assez!

PETER. Oh Christ! That's all she gave
me . . . can't you . . .

*He reluctantly but hastily pulls out
some more money. The man takes the
note with a look of annoyance and
starts pawing over the cash register
trying to find the change.*

*The noise of a train moving out of
the station as a further whistle goes.*

Keep the change.

*He lifts the heavy wadge and pushing
past the queue is about to move out
of shot.*

*Somebody in the front of the queue
calls at him and waves a couple of
magazines he's has left behind.*

Forget it!

*He runs back towards the barrier
across the main hall, dodging people
as he goes. A luggage 'train' rattles
past as he nears the barrier. Whistles
are blowing loudly. We track fast
behind him as he comes up to the
barrier. The ticket collectors have
shut the barrier and wave at him that
he is too late, but he confidently*

*pushes past them and gives the barrier
a shove. It swings open on the second
attempt. He runs up to the train, his
manner confident, not desperate,
though highly annoyed. A couple more
magazines drop onto the platform as
he runs. People lean from the train, a
couple of kids, and shout down at
him, encouraging him. He climbs
aboard the train amid much shrieking
and whistles.*

4. Interior. Train corridor. Afternoon.

*The first thing Peter sees as he climbs
onto the train, is three of the German
eighteen-year-old boys who he had
seen running across the tracks earlier.
They are the only people in the corridor.
The leader of these three, Dietrich, is a
boy of immense nervous energy, with
bright blue eyes, charismatic looks and a
very loud voice.*

*Dietrich stares at him as he moves down
the corridor and into the compartment.*

5. Interior. Train. Afternoon.

*Peter slips back the glass door and enters
the compartment. Frau Messner looks up.*

FRAU MESSNER (*polite smile*): You see.
You did have time.

*The train is pulling out of the
station: the noise of its lumbering
across the points outside the station.*

PETER. All the time in the world . . .

PRESTON. You must have gone to the
wrong bookstall.

*Peter hands her the huge pile of
magazines.*

FRAU MESSNER. Thank you. That was
so kind of you. (*Very slight pause, then
she glances up.*) Was there any change for
me? Do you have my change?

*Peter has remained standing, facing
her, keeping his balance as the train
begins to pick up speed.*

PETER. Not exactly. You didn't give me nearly enough in fact.

FRAU MESSNER. I didn't give you enough money? (*Concerned tone.*) I must give you some more at once. Immediately. (*She shuffles in her bag.*) Oh. I only have this! (*She is holding a large banknote – looking straight back at him.*) Can you change me a one thousand schilling note? This is all I've got. I'm afraid all my change has completely gone. (*To the rest of the compartment:*) You have to give away so much money all the time now.

The note is stretched out towards Peter. He stares at it.

PETER. No, I can't.

FRAU MESSNER (*innocent*): What are we going to do?

A very slight pause. Preston watching.

PETER (*sharp*): It's all right, we'll forget it, for the moment. (*He sits as the train jolts on and then begins to run more smoothly.*)

PRESTON. They're off on time for once! Only fifty seconds late. They'll never keep it up.

FRAU MESSNER (*checking her magazines*): And you've got *almost* all of them – that is good.

PETER (*glances up at Lorraine, opposite him*): I'm exhausted. I haven't run like that for years.

LORRAINE. You've still got your seat though haven't you?

The afternoon sun is on Lorraine as she lies back in her seat staring at him.

Preston suddenly leaning towards Frau Messner.

Shot of the Belgian countryside through the window in the afternoon light.

PRESTON. The coffee of course will cost a fortune on this train. And it'll be undrinkable. Don't bother to try it.

Peter looks back at Lorraine as Preston's voice continues – Peter's eyes half close then open.

(*Voice-over.*) On the boat, just now, how much do you think I paid for a cup of coffee, like that, no bigger than a matchbox, with a piece of green icing on the top, and a packet of peanuts. How much?

FRAU MESSNER (*voice over*): How much? You tell me?

PRESTON (*voice-over*): No you have to have a guess.

Peter's eyes wander across Lorraine's body, up her legs, her blouse, the buttons slightly undone, her brown neck, the long smooth hair – up to her face. Afternoon light. He closes his eyes, as the train really picks up speed.

The screen goes to black as the noise of the train becomes much louder, hurtling forward.

Dim shapes of other passengers from Peter's point of view begin to come into focus. Preston's voice burbling on.

Then onto Peter's eyes, as they open.

It is evening now, stormy sun-light outside.

Peter's point of view. The camera pans up the pair of legs in front of him, up the stockings, up the skirt, up to the face. Frau Messner is staring back at him with a polite smile, sitting in Lorraine's seat.

Peter's head swings round. Lorraine is sitting in Frau Messner's seat, staring into the corridor. Silence: as he stares at Frau Messner.

The sound of the train cracking along.

FRAU MESSNER. She let me change places. Wasn't it kind of her. (*There is a steely gleam in her eye. A close-up of the pile of magazines completely untouched.*) It makes me feel a lot better.

PETER (*sharp*): Good . . .

The sound of a bell ringing down the corridor and the sound of somebody calling for bookings for dinner – his voice is some way off still.

FRAU MESSNER. Have you had a good sleep?

PETER. I was only asleep a moment.

FRAU MESSNER. Oh no. (*Looking at him.*) You were asleep for a long time. Nearly an hour. Maybe more.

PETER. Really? I don't believe you.

He glances at Lorraine who is looking out of the window.

FRAU MESSNER (*not looking away*): Are you going a long way?

PETER (*reluctantly*): Yes – I am.

FRAU MESSNER. So am I. I'm going all the way to Wien. I will be here the whole journey.

PETER (*smiles to himself*): I imagined as much.

He glances towards Lorraine who is still staring out into the corridor.

The door flies open and the steward is flourishing a handful of red tickets.

FRAU MESSNER. No I don't want any.

PETER. Merci.

The steward flicks him a ticket.

LORRAINE. Could I also . . .

The steward flicks her a ticket and is out of the compartment in seconds, pushing the door loudly shut behind him.

While Frau Messner speaks Kellner is adding something on a pocket calculator; Preston is staring ahead with a glazed expression.

FRAU MESSNER (*to the whole compartment*): I have brought my own food. I always travel with my own, somebody prepares it for me. I never go anywhere without them. Little chickens cooked in bread crumbs. (*Slowly:*) Since before the war, since I

was only small, I have always travelled with them. (*She indicates a delicious looking pile of food in a wooden basket covered in silver foil.*)

PRESTON. Quite right – the dining cars on these trains are hell on earth. You feel much worse when you come out than when you go in. Also, you can get bad food poisoning. Dreadful.

FRAU MESSNER (*she smiles*): Like everything, it gets worse. (*Pulling her money out of her purse.*) I just have to count this now. (*The train is really rattling along. Frau Messner turns and looks at Kellner.*) You don't mind if I turn my back on you for a moment, I just must see how much I've got left. (*She starts to count the money.*)

KELLNER (*smiles, a broad, food-humoured smile*): No please, don't mind me. I'm used to the sound of money. I hear it every day from seven o'clock in the morning. (*He grins.*) Every day except Sundays – then I hear it at home.

A close-up of banknotes going through Frau Messner's fingers, Peter watches her count, as he takes out a packet of cigarettes and puts a cigarette in his mouth. As the cigarette actually goes into his mouth Frau Messner looks up.

FRAU MESSNER (*very firmly, smiles*): Do you think if you want to smoke, you could smoke outside in the passage.

Peter looks up in astonishment.

If you could go into the passage because we're going a long way, I asked for a non-smoker but for some reason this seems to be a smoker.

PETER. That's unfortunate. (*Icy.*) But if you don't like it I suggest you find somewhere else to sit.

FRAU MESSNER (*ignoring this completely*): I think the whole carriage must be a non-smoker. I'm sure it says so on the tickets.

PETER. I'm afraid it doesn't.

FRAU MESSNER. You don't have to go far — the passage is just out there.

Lorraine gets up and walks into the corridor. She does not turn round but stands with her back to them.

PETER. And what happens to me if I don't?

Frau Messner looks back at him. He lights the cigarette.

FRAU MESSNER (*still staring at him*): Neither of these gentlemen are smokers, you see.

PRESTON. No. On a long journey it can get unpleasant. One wakes up at night with ash all over one's body.

Peter blows smoke across the room.

FRAU MESSNER (*sharp*): When I was young the men always smoked in the passage. They used to stay out there the whole journey — hanging their heads out of the window.

PETER. Did they?

FRAU MESSNER (*politely*): I am not going to ask you again.

Peter, surprised at this, glances out at Lorraine in the passage, then straight into Frau Messner's eyes.

PETER. I'll be back in a second.

6. Interior. Train corridor. Afternoon.

Peter goes out into the corridor. He glances back through the glass. Frau Messner is back sorting her money. He turns in surprise to look at the corridor. It is now chocker-block, mostly kids, some standing up or sitting on their suitcases, or the small side-seats. They stare back at Peter. At the end of the carriage he can see Lorraine standing by the end window that stares directly onto the track.

Peter moves down the corridor, picking his way amongst the kids, we see the fat man sitting all alone. The blinds are pulled down, but Peter catches

a glimpse through a gap in the blinds. In another compartment girls have stretched their legs out, kicked their shoes off, and are already fast asleep.

Halfway down the passage Dietrich is leaning up against the wall, smoking, talking loudly in German. Two English schoolgirls with podgy white faces are sitting on their suitcase near Dietrich.

Peter reaches Lorraine at the end window. They stand next to each other for this sequence staring directly out, the train moving fast along a curving scenic track.

PETER (*moving up to her*): I think this is going to end in tears.

LORRAINE (*not looking at him*): How do you mean?

PETER. I can't sit there with her behaving like that. (*He smiles.*) I really might hit her — do her an injury.

LORRAINE. She's just old, you don't have to worry.

PETER. I'm going to have to find another seat.

LORRAINE (*still in profile, not looking at him*): You'll never find another one. The whole train's chocker-block.

Peter stares at the people on suitcases, in jeans, pale faces, holding beer cans, Dietrich is holding forth in rapid German. One of the other kids blows the football whistle loudly.

PETER. Where did they all suddenly spring from?

LORRAINE. You were asleep.

PETER. I had no idea it would be so full. They must be all going home. They don't look particularly cheerful.

LORRAINE (*glancing back*): Why are they making so much noise?

PETER. We must be getting near the German Border. (*Turning back to Lorraine.*) I should have flown. I nearly always do fly everywhere. (*An ironic smile as the kids lark around in the back of the shot.*) I wanted a change.

LORRAINE (*staring out of the window*): There you are then.

PETER (*more urgent*): I can't sit with that old woman any more. I've really got to find another seat.

LORRAINE. It's totally impossible.

PETER. Come on – we could try. (*He takes her sleeve.*)

LORRAINE (*suddenly looking at him. Slight smile*): You could.

PETER (*surprised*): Yes.

Lorraine turns back to the window. Peter glances at her face, her blouse.

LORRAINE. It's going to rain. It's hardly stopped raining since I've been in Europe. First in England and now here. On and on.

Dietrich suddenly shouts at them, in German, teasingly lewdly down the length of the corridor.

What's he saying?

PETER. I don't know.

Lorraine moves away from him back down the corridor. Peter follows her. They stand in the corridor next to their own compartment, next to Dietrich in the corridor.

Peter glances at Frau Messner. She is leaning back in her seat, seemingly sleeping, but then she looks up for a second straight at him.

(*Suddenly louder to Lorraine.*) Why on earth did you give up your seat for her?

LORRAINE. Because she really needed it so badly.

PETER. Don't you realise that's exactly what she wanted to happen?

LORRAINE. No it wasn't.

PETER. What do you mean?

LORRAINE (*looks at him*): She wanted *your* seat. (*Straight at him.*) And you should have given it to her – you really should.

PETER. Why? Why should people like that get exactly what they want all the time? It's what she's used to.

LORRAINE. It was rude of you. She's an old lady.

Peter stares at Frau Messner through the glass. As he talks about her the camera moves across Frau Messner's face.

PETER. Do you think she knows, we're talking about her?

LORRAINE. She looks like she's dozing.

PETER. Yes . . . she can probably hear everything we're saying. No doubt she can hear perfectly through glass. I expect she can hear through reinforced concrete. She's obviously not going to forgive me for the whole trip. (*He smiles.*) For defying her.

Frau Messner moves in her seat but does not open her eyes.

BOY (*in broken English, to both of them*): Have you . . . a cigarette?

He seems very nervous, preoccupied, flicking his hair away from his face.

PETER. Yes. O.K. Here.

BOY. Thank you.

PETER (*smiling at his nervousness*): You can have two or three if you like?

The Boy takes them and goes into the compartment on the right-hand side of theirs and sits by the door. Peter can see him through the glass.

(*Softer to Lorraine.*) Maybe I'll go and explore on my own then.

Shot of Frau Messner sleeping through the glass.

LORRAINE (*slight smile*): You could always get off the train couldn't you – if you don't like being here.

PETER. No I can't. I've got to be in Linz at ten o'clock tomorrow. (*He smiles, jokey.*) I could pull the communication cord and get her taken off.

LORRAINE. What cord?

PETER (*points*): There. The lever. (*They look up at it. Peter stretches up to it.*) This actually is much more difficult to pull than you think. They're very stiff. You have to really tug at them. (*Peter touches it with the tip of his finger.*) It's sticky.

As he touches it, the train brakes savagely. They are all thrown violently sideways in the passage.

LORRAINE. What's happening? Did you do that?

PETER (*smiles*): Unfortunately, no. We've reached the border. (*He pulls out his passport.*) Passport checks and everything.

The train brakes again. A loud whining screech. The noise cuts out and then returns three times until the train finally comes to a halt.

Sounds as if it's in pain doesn't it?

As the train is stopping Lorraine takes Peter's passport.

LORRAINE. Can I see?

The rain starts during the following speech, streaking down the window.

Very hard rain playing on the roof and spattering down the window.

A shot of guards moving down the track outside the train.

Peter bending over his passport as she looks at it: charming smile.

PETER. I work for a publishers. Public relations. Coaxing successful authors out of bed and on to television. Not that they really need encouragement of course. Some of them get incredibly nervous. I have to pour drink down them in the taxi.

The door at the end of the carriage slides open with a crash. Border guards in uniform, glistening mackintosh capes, move through. They wear guns. They begin to check passports at the other end of the

train. One is very young. The other an old man in his sixties.

These are the Belgians. Then we're in Germany.

Dietrich suddenly snatches Peter's passport. Another kid takes it, and it is returned to him in a flash.

DIETRICH (*grins at Peter*): You like to see my pictures. (*He produces photographs and presses them up to Peter's face.*) My parents. (*Pictures of prosperous Germans with Mercedes.*) My car . . . and me taking drugs. (*A picture of Dietrich sitting on a wall inhaling something through his nose.*) I'll show this one to the Police.

Peter: slight uneasy smile as the photographs are whipped away from him as the guards get up to Dietrich. Dietrich waves the picture of himself taking drugs in the guards' faces as they look at his passport, and jabbers in German. They take no notice as he does this.

Peter notices the young guard pull back the door of the fat man's compartment.

The rain is much louder, beating on the roof and down the sides of the train.

The fat man is clearly visible hunched up in a large black overcoat. His compartment looks empty though Peter can only see half of it through the glass.

PETER. I think he's all alone in there you know. Got the whole compartment to himself! I wonder how.

He glances at the kids sitting on the suitcases in the passage. The guards are picking their way amongst them.

Pan with his point of view across his own compartment – with Frau Messner looking up.

(*Voice-over.*) Maybe if we're very lucky they'll send her back to Ostend.

Across to the right-hand side of the compartment he can see the Boy who asked for a cigarette sitting restlessly by the door nervously chain-smoking, lighting the second cigarette with the end of the first. Slight track in on him as Peter stares at him fascinated. The Boy's face is extremely tense and scared.

PETER. Look at that boy there.

LORRAINE. Which boy?

Close up of the boy's face.

PETER (*voice-over*): There.

LORRAINE (*voice-over*): Why?

PETER (*voice-over*): He's frightened, I think.

LORRAINE (*quietly*): Look — his socks don't match.

YOUNG GUARD (*pushes up to Peter*): Passport . . . (*He glances at Peter and snaps his passport, returning it.*) Merci . . .

The young guard then pushes back the door of the compartment the boy is in and stands over him. Real close-up, through the glass, of the boy's face. We see the panic and his effort to stop it showing. The boy looks at the floor. The young guard is about to give back the passport, when he suddenly stops himself, and looks closely. The boy is almost biting on his cigarette.

YOUNG GUARD (*sharp*): Ce passport n'est pas le votre.

BOY (*without real conviction*): C'est le mien.

The young guard talks to him rapidly. It is only half-audible from where Peter watches.

YOUNG GUARD. Venez ici.

He takes the boy and leads him out into the corridor. The boy begins to babble, people stand up in the carriage half-obscuring Peter's view.

PETER. I told you.

The young guard calls sharply to the older guard to join him, and then places the boy up against the window and frisks him.

The rain is playing loudly on the roof.

Someone in the passage is cat-calling, but quite sheepishly. The boy's face is sullen, but anxious.

OLD GUARD (*moves up to Peter and Lorraine*): Could you move into your seats please! Take your seats.

Lorraine and Peter remain in the corridor.

The boy's head goes back and suddenly he starts shouting, though it is unintelligible.

7. Interior. Train compartment. Afternoon.

Peter watching from the corridor.

FRAU MESSNER (*looking up*): What's happening? Why are we being held up?

PRESTON. No doubt it's a forged passport. I've heard it often happens. Maybe he was not meant to leave the country — in trouble with the courts.

Peter is watching the boy who is near to tears. The older guard has left urgently, the young guard is standing with the boy, holding him firmly by one arm.

The boy has sat down in the passage, by just letting his legs sink under him and the young guard is pulling him to his feet and dragging him along the corridor.

PETER (*to Lorraine*): He looks just like I used to when I was being taken back to boarding school.

The boy passes Peter, his face very close to him.

FRAU MESSNER (*watches the boy as he goes by*): He doesn't look well.

KELLNER (*suddenly very sharp and*

impatient): It is annoying to be kept waiting, isn't it? We must make up a lot of time now or we'll be very late. (*He glances at his watch, tense.*) Come on . . . It has to start now . . .

From Peter's point of view we see, through the train window, the boy being led across the railway lines against a large, dwarfing, industrial back-drop, towards waiting police cars.

As they cross the lines the boy pulls half-heartedly away. Dietrich and other kids cat-calling from the train. When they are half-way across the lines Dietrich suddenly opens the door of the train and jumps out, racing across the lines towards them, shouting exuberantly in German. The police stop and shout threateningly back at him. Dietrich mockingly raises his hands above his head, taunting them as he does so, then runs back towards the train for all he is worth, as the other kids cheer him and laugh, and the train begins to move.

Dietrich grinning, leans against the passage wall looking flustered and excited. His eyes meet Peter's.

DIETRICH. Some fun eh?

Cut to over-head shot of the train speeding deeper into Germany.

The door of the compartment slides back and a small man in a mackintosh enters. Water dripping off him. He moves towards the last seat.

The compartment is now full and claustrophobic. It is now night outside.

PRESTON. Excuse me, that seat has been reserved by somebody. Are you that person?

The man nods and sits next to Peter, facing Frau Messner and Kellner. His face is round, very white and flabby, and totally expressionless. He grunts at them, a hardly audible noise.

He takes off his mackintosh and rolls it up into a ball. Muddy water leaks off it and runs across the floor towards Frau Messner, who slides her feet backwards and starts lifting her hand luggage off the floor and onto her lap and the seat. She stops for a second as she realises something is missing and begins to sort through bags, getting more alarmed as she does so.

Peter watches her. As her panic begins to spread the noise of her wrestling with her bags fills the compartment.

FRAU MESSNER. My food . . . my picnic . . . (*She looks up.*) The poussins. It's vanished. They've gone.

PRESTON. They can't have done. Maybe they have fallen down the side here.

Preston pushes his hand down the side of the seat.

FRAU MESSNER (*very concerned*): They were here! I fell asleep for a few moments. Just a moment. And now they have gone.

Kellner and Lorraine begin to look, Lorraine round her feet.

It was in a basket, all done up in silver paper. Everything I had for the whole journey. You all saw it – I showed it to you.

KELLNER. I'll look up here.

He looks in the luggage rack. The small man lifts his mackintosh. Everybody moves except Peter.

PRESTON (*to Kellner*): Here, lift up the seat – let's have a look underneath here.

They look underneath the seat. Just a few coins and a dirty magazine that have slipped down the seat stare back at them.

Lorraine and the small man in the mackintosh have moved into the corridor to allow more room.

Waved on by Preston, Lorraine stands with her face right up to the glass staring into the compartment watching

Peter throughout the rest of the sequence. He glances at her with a knowing smile half-way through the sequence.

As Kellner and Preston have been lifting the seat, Frau Messner carries straight on.

FRAU MESSNER. Chicken legs in bread-crumbs and Wurst. They were prepared for me specially. I have never travelled anywhere without them. We must find them.

She suddenly stops and looks at Peter, who has not moved at all. He is sitting watching her.

(*Quiet.*) Have you seen any of them?

PETER (*with an amused smile, staring back at her*): I haven't seen any of your chicken, no.

FRAU MESSNER (*staring at him*): In silver paper. It was wrapped in . . .

PETER. I know. I still haven't seen them.

The others all stop and look at him. Silence as the train rattles on. The rain is still streaking the window. Peter glances at Lorraine who is staring at him icily.

FRAU MESSNER (*staring down at Peter*): They didn't run away by themselves.

PETER. I wouldn't be so sure.

FRAU MESSNER (*into his face*): Could you just stand up for a moment please.

PETER. I don't think so.

FRAU MESSNER (*her voice sharper*): I just want you to stand up and show me. I won't be angry if they are here.

PETER (*a slight smile*): Are you doubting my word. (*Pause.*) Maybe you haven't lost them at all.

FRAU MESSNER (*very forcefully*): I will not be angry with you, if you've been hiding them. Just stand up now.

Peter stands up. They all crane forward to see: there is nothing there.

PETER (*smiles*): Of course, I could have swallowed it all already. Could be inside me.

He touches his stomach. They are both standing up.

FRAU MESSNER (*a piercing look*): I shall ask you just once — have you taken my food?

A shot of the others watching Peter.

PETER. No I have not.

A bell goes down the passage and we hear the voice of a steward.

(*He smiles.*) Why should I — I have a ticket for the dining car. (*He waves it.*) Now if you'll excuse me.

He glances at Lorraine, and smiles as he moves out of the compartment into the corridor.

I'll see you in there!

Lorraine has sat down again at the edge of the compartment, her face registering disapproval at his behaviour. She glances straight at him and then away, their eyes meet for a second.

FRAU MESSNER (*as Peter is leaving*): I won't ask to see his bag. We must believe he's telling the truth. I will just sit here all night with nothing to eat.

Peter closes the door shut on this last line and stares back through the glass for a second.

Dietrich has been standing in the passage. The three other German boys, his friends, are further down the corridor amongst the other kids. Dietrich is standing by the two puffy faced schoolgirls who are shyly sitting on their suitcases.

Dietrich looking at Peter as he comes out of the compartment, his manner is loud, volatile.

DIETRICH. Are you an American? I think you're American.

PETER (*as he passes him, glancing back at Frau Messner*): Hardly, no.

DIETRICH (*pulling the cigarette out of his own mouth*): This is an American cigarette. (*Glancing down at his sneakers.*) This is American shoe, I think you're American.

He turns away and starts talking excitedly in German to his friends down the carriage, laughing and raising his voice.

Peter has moved down the corridor towards the dining car.

8. Interior. Corridors. Night.

The corridor is lit by wall lamps — not very brightly. It is night outside. The train is travelling very fast. People are still sitting on suitcases. Beer cans are rattling on the floor.

The door of the fat man's compartment is slightly ajar, the blinds are drawn down. Peter on a sudden impulse pushes back the door and steps in.

The fat man is sitting hunched up in his coat. The compartment is totally empty: he has covered the seats with objects, radio-cassette recorder, brief-cases, etc., to make it look occupied.

PETER. I'm sorry . . . I didn't realise . . .

FAT MAN (*waving him away. In broken English*): Full up. This is full up. They're all in the dining car, they will be back in a moment. They're just coming back.

Peter grins to himself, leaves the compartment and glances at the kids sitting in the corridor. He moves on towards the door. There is a loud sound outside: heavy industrial noise. Peter stops by the window and stares out, a red glow on his face.

Cut to outside exterior. Shots of a vast steel works, a huge industrial complex flooded by arc lights.

Cut back to Peter as he is about to

move out of the corridor. There is a noise behind him. He stares back along the corridor. Frau Messner is following him down the corridor, walking sharply towards him.

PETER (*under his breath*): Oh my God.

He walks through the next carriage. It has an aisle down the middle and no compartments.

The carriage is full of people lying sprawled over the seats asleep, or just staring ahead or playing cards. A transistor is on somewhere but the sound is terrible, bottles are stacked up on the table. Nobody is talking.

Peter walks down the carriage. As he is about to leave Frau Messner appears at the other end of the carriage and moves towards him.

He goes through the doors. There is a connecting bridge section into the next part of the train, joining the carriages together. We can hear the noise of the tracks, it is deafening. The floor moves underfoot.

Peter crosses over gingerly for the train is moving fast. As soon as he has crossed the doors open behind him.

Frau Messner stands on the other side of the bridge section staring across at him.

(*Peter has to raise his voice above the crushing noise of the train.*) Where are you going?

FRAU MESSNER. I am going to have my dinner.

PETER. You can't. You need a ticket.

He waves his red ticket.

FRAU MESSNER (*stares at him and produces the red ticket*): I have one.

PETER. How on earth did you get that?

FRAU MESSNER. The young girl gave it to me.

A close-up of Peter, complete surprise on his face. He turns to go. She stands on the other side of the bridge section and then moves to cross it. It is wobbling around considerably. She looks at him, but Peter does not move to help her.

For a moment Frau Messner stands stranded and has to clutch to remain upright.

Peter reluctantly stretches out his hand. Frau Messner crosses. She walks past him into the bar.

9. Interior. Bar. Night.

The bar area is small and crammed with people, the air is full of smoke.
It is impossible to get to the bar. There is a queue and people are leaning against it – kids and an old man.
Frau Messner walks straight through, pushing past people. Peter follows, letting her get out of sight. He glances at the faces of the kids in the bar. One girl is curled up in the corner, on the floor. She is wearing heavy eye shadow and looks very drunk. Somebody is singing a song in the background: a pop song with German and American words muddled together.
Peter moves through the bar into the dining car.

10. Interior. Dining car. Night.

The dining car is covered in mahogany panelling and has low-hung lamps. Each table has a vase with three carnations in it. There are only about nine tables and they are all full, except for one small table half way down the carriage opposite the sideboard. Frau Messner is standing over this table.

FRAU MESSNER. I will sit here.

She sits with much clatter and moving of chairs.

PETER. Goodbye then.

There are no other tables.

Peter glances across the whole dining car, there are some students huddled in groups and some older people eating in silence. Hardly anybody has any food – there is one scraggy salad on the sideboard.

At the far end of the carriage, leaning against the door, stands a large man staring back down the aisle.

You would have thought there would have been just one more free table.

FRAU MESSNER (looking up, having settled herself): You are still here? Where are you going to sit? I suppose you can sit here. But maybe you would prefer to stand.

PETER (smiles): Yes, I think, maybe I would.

FRAU MESSNER. Do as you wish. (She looks with disgust at some used plates that have been left on the table.) Really they should have cleared these things. I will have to call them.

The waiter, a very small, dapper man, with an ability to walk down the carriage without catching anybody's eye. moves straight down the aisle very fast and disappears.

Are you going to stand there the whole meal? If the train stops suddenly you will probably get your neck broken.

The train is travelling very fast.

PETER (staring down at her): I think I'll take the chance.

FRAU MESSNER. We're coming soon to a station, a big city.

The train lurches and Peter topples forward slightly. Frau Messner watches unmoved.

After the lurching the train need not be going very fast. We see the lights of the city looming up, moving past the window.

Peter slides into the seat opposite her, the carnations between them.

Exterior shot of Peter sitting opposite Frau Messner in the dining car, beginning very close on the window, and pulling away to show the whole lighted carriage, sliding into the city, with kids hanging their heads out of the window.

(*Matter-of-fact.*) There! I can keep a watch on you. (*She glances round.*) Now, we have no menus as you can see. (*She points at a group of kids over on the other side of the carriage.*) Can you get theirs? – They don't need them anymore.

PETER (*not moving*): Why can't you do it?

FRAU MESSNER (*slight smile*): Because I think you're nearer.

Peter is not.

I don't think you can be very hungry.

Peter stretches for the menus. In doing so he notices the man standing leaning against the door at the far end of the carriage. He is staring down the aisle. The man is watching everything that is going on with a distant smile on his face.

PETER (*dropping the menus in front of her*): There you are, and that is absolutely all I'm doing.

FRAU MESSNER (*glances at a menu for a second and then snaps it shut*): There is nothing I can eat here, I don't think, they will have to prepare me something else.

Peter lights up a cigarette and looks at her through the carnations.

She moves the flowers.

Tell me what is your name? Do you have one?

PETER. Yes.

He smokes and looks at her.

FRAU MESSNER (*watching his eyes move*): My name is Frau Messner. (*Very slowly.*) Can you say that? Mess-ner.

PETER. No I don't think I can.

FRAU MESSNER. I think you ought to try. English children can never speak any languages.

The waiter rushes straight past them not looking to right or left.

(*Sharply.*) Muchte ich . . .

The waiter walks straight past.

He is not attending. (*Frau Messner lowers her voice and leans towards Peter.*) Look – you can see that girl's bosoms. You can see them quite clearly. (*She is looking at a girl who is wearing a tight fitting T-shirt.*) I don't think all these people are meant to be here. They can't all have tickets to eat here! (*Her voice getting really loud.*)

They have to have a ticket like this – a red *ticket.*

PETER. Do you have to talk so loudly, everybody can hear you? You really should have travelled first class shouldn't you?

FRAU MESSNER. First class. How I could possibly afford it? It's so expensive.

Peter looks down at the discreet but rich jewellery on her fingers and round her neck.

Frau Messner moves her head suddenly, looking round, her restlessness beginning to grow.

They have tried to make it look like an old carriage. You see? (*She indicates panelling.*) Before the war these dining carriages were so beautiful. They had fresh salmon here you know, lying here, and sometimes sturgeon. They have tried to make the carriages look old but none of it is real. It's all false. See this table? It's plastic.

She suddenly stabs at the panelling with her fork, and rubs the fork up and down the table.

You see! You can't scratch it. I can't scratch it at all. It's all false.

The fork makes a loud screeching noise on the table.

PETER (*looking away, embarrassed*): Please, can we sit here with no trouble! Please.

The waiter passes down the aisle.

FRAU MESSNER (*loudly to him*): Warum haben sie uns nicht bedient.

He walks straight past her. Others are trying to get his attention, but he ignores all of them.

Did you see that? He didn't even stop.

PETER. No.

FRAU MESSNER (*extremely restless*): Next time he passes we will *stop* him. It is a disgrace this is still here. (*Indicating the dirty plates.*) Why are you pulling all the flowers to pieces?

PETER. Only one of them – (*He looks at her through the flowers which he has moved back.*) It makes me less tense.

FRAU MESSNER (*quiet*): Pick it up.

Peter puts it in his buttonhole.

You are well dressed for a young man nowadays. (*She feels his jacket.*) This would be expensive. (*She looks straight at him.*) Are you doing something important?

PETER. Could be?

FRAU MESSNER. Where are you going?

She is looking directly at him, impassive.

PETER (*looks at her*): I'm going to a bookfair in Linz, hundreds of shiny new books. They sell books like cars now.

FRAU MESSNER (*still staring at him*): And it is important?

Peter smiles slightly, watching her warily.

Cut to the lights of the city, growing in intensity and size.

(*Looking straight at him.*) Is it important?

PETER (*a slight smile*): Very, as it happens. I've got to meet two famous authors that we handle. Big European celebrities . . . medium-sized celebrities, 10.30 tomorrow morning. It's the first time I've represented my firm abroad. (*Slight smile to himself.*) Naturally if I handle things well . . . (*Suddenly he looks up.*) You're *not* listening to me. You ask me questions and then you don't even bother to listen.

FRAU MESSNER. I heard enough.

She is looking about, extremely agitated.

I have to find the waiter. I can't wait any longer!

The waiter approaches with food, and walks straight past them as Frau Messner calls out to him.

He didn't even look at me. Stop him.

The waiter gives the food to a group of students. The train is beginning to slow down and draw into a station.

(*Leaning forward.*) Were those people here before or after us? I think they were here after. I am quite sure they haven't got the tickets. We should ask them. They aren't allowed to eat if they haven't. Will you ask them if they have dinner tickets? Go on.

PETER. Don't be ridiculous . . .

Frau Messner immediately leans over and asks them: half-audible.

FRAU MESSNER. They say they have. But they must be lying.

PETER (*staring at the man who is watching the carriage. He has not moved at all*): He's watching you – you'll get us both thrown out any moment. I wonder who he is.

FRAU MESSNER (*matter-of-factly*): A policeman – secret policeman.

PETER. He's hardly very secret. He can't be a policeman. (*Peter stares fascinated. The man has one hand in his pocket.*) Maybe he's the chef . . .

FRAU MESSNER (*wrestling in her seat, unable to sit any more*): I can't bear this any longer. We will show them. There's a salad over there. (*She indicates the miserable salad.*) You could reach it if you tried. (*She stares at him.*) Why don't you try? Go on.

PETER. No.

Shot of the man, watching.

FRAU MESSNER (*staring at him*): You can reach it from your seat easily.

PETER. You really can't wait for anything can you? It's like a disease. I have never ever seen somebody quite so unable to wait their turn. It's almost as if the effort would kill you.

FRAU MESSNER (*stares at him for a moment. Quietly*): If you are going to be rude to me you can leave my table. (*Her tone changes, still quiet.*) I *cannot* wait. Ever. They have to give you service, that is what they are paid to do.

The waiter moves down the aisle, still not looking at any of his customers, his dapper figure moving fast.

Here he comes now. We will catch him.

As he passes her Frau Messner catches the waiter by the arm. The drink he is carrying spills. She holds him by the arm while remaining seated in her chair.

Wir haben zu lange gewartet.

The waiter whose arm is being held, is very quiet.

WAITER. Bitte . . .

Everybody is watching. The conversation fades until the carriage is completely silent. The train has stopped.

PETER. Please, could you not . . .

He is looking at the tablecloth in embarrassment.

FRAU MESSNER (*very sharply*): Werde Ihnen anmelden. (*To Peter.*) I am going to report him. Give me a pencil please.

She is still holding on to the waiter. Peter is watching in amazement.

(*Really sharply.*) Come on, have you got a pencil, will you give it to me.

PETER (*quietly*): I haven't got a pencil and I won't give it to you.

FRAU MESSNER. I am holding him here until I have taken his name.

She looks in her own bag with one hand. The waiter hands her a pencil sharply. The large man at the end of the aisle has not moved at all and is watching. The waiter stands frozen.

Wie heissen sie?

WAITER. Rutz.

FRAU MESSNER (*writes it down*): Rutz.

The waiter immediately moves away. Frau Messner picks up the dirty plates and holds them out across the gangway.

(*Calling after him.*) Warum haben sie diese sachen nicht wegenommen?

The waiter ignores her and disappears, leaving her still holding the dirty dishes.

Frau Messner simply lets go of the dishes and they shatter in the gangway, pieces of crockery going everywhere.

And now I will go.

She gets up and walks out of the dining car. The dining car is very silent.

Peter crouches down to begin picking up pieces of crockery: Everybody is staring at him. He looks embarrassed. He puts part of the broken plate on his chair and leaves the dining car.

11. Interior. Corridor. Night.

Frau Messner is standing by the door of the carriage, as if expecting him to follow her. As soon as he appears she starts talking loudly.

FRAU MESSNER (*firmly*): You have to make these people understand you. See that when they do wrong, they will be punished, and then they will never forget it. You just have to do it.

PETER. It was a totally ridiculous thing to do and now I can't get any supper. (*He glances back to the dining car.*) I am quite incredibly hungry.

Frau Messner is by the door trying to open it.

Where are you going?

FRAU MESSNER. The train is stopping here. They have left the handle off this door — it won't open! There should be a handle.

PETER. You can't even open the doors. Haven't you ever learnt how to do this? You've probably always had doors opened for you!

He moves to the door and slides down the window.

FRAU MESSNER. It stops here half-an-hour. I will find something to eat in the station.

She opens the door and moves to climb out.

I can show you where you can eat. Can you hold this?

PETER (*staring at Frau Messner. Slight smile*): No, thanks.

FRAU MESSNER. Are you hungry or not? Do as you wish.

She climbs out of the train. Close up of Peter looking famished. He stares back towards the dining car. The waiter is still standing outside the dining car looking at him with extreme hostility.

12. Exterior. Platform. Frankfurt. Night.

Cut to outside the train. Frau Messner is walking down the outside of the train. Peter is behind her walking very slowly.

PETER. How do you know the train stops here half an hour?

FRAU MESSNER. You should have a piece of paper. It tells you all the times.

PETER (*walking several paces behind her*): Are you completely sure? You're positive it's half an hour?

FRAU MESSNER. At least half an hour.

PETER (*looking to check on his ticket*): We've got to keep in sight of the train.

He glances back. One or two people have got off the train and are standing on the platform having a smoke.

FRAU MESSNER (*quietly*): I am not interested if you come or not.

Receding shot of people on the platform.

The locomotive towers above Peter. He stares up at the cab. A small boy stares back through the windscreen of the cab: a hard, very white face. He is the only person in the cab.

PETER. I hope he hasn't been driving us.

They walk past a chauffeur standing with a pile of suitcases next to him. A fur coat is lying on top of the suitcases.

FRAU MESSNER (*waves at it*): The money people have now . . .

They walk across the huge concourse of Frankfurt Station.

There are powerful lights shining down. There is a large puddle of water on the concourse, although it is a totally covered area.

Frau Messner is walking purposefully in front of him and skirts the edge of the puddle.

The roof leaks of course.

Peter stares around him at the large bright advertisements lit up along the wall. A receding shot of the front of the engine.

Peter is staring around him. There are no signs telling him which station it is.

PETER. Which city are we in anyway?

Frau Messner is walking across the station. He follows, a short way behind her, staring at her back at her determined walk.

13. Exterior. Station concourse. Night.

Along the edge of the walls of the huge concourse are some kids, lying in sleeping bags. Some are leaning against the wall smoking and watching them as they pass.

FRAU MESSNER (*glancing over to them*): They are probably all from good families.

Peter stares at their pale faces. They stare right back at him: a glazed look.

PETER. It's funny how people are attracted to stations.

The kids are leaning up against huge lighted advertisements and some posters for some local elections.

(*As he moves past them*): Some people live for years in places like this, sleeping out here. Maybe they're going to try to jump a train.

The faces stare back at him, some of them are very young, staring out of the tops of sleeping bags.

A blond-haired boy is leaning against the wall with a guitar, half strumming it, singing an old sixties standard, singing a few English words, humming the rest.

The kids are a mixture of long-haired boys and much younger, more aggressive-looking kids. Two young girls with very short haircuts are leaning against a wall.

We see these kids as Frau Messner walks purposefully across the great hall of the station. We track with Peter, just a pace behind her.

(*Glancing up at the enormous clock.*) I'm taking regular time checks.

Frau Messner is striding ahead.

Where on earth are you going?

FRAU MESSNER (*not waiting for him*): I know where we can eat.

PETER. We've already been three minutes.

14. Exterior. Side entrance. Night.

We cut to them moving through the underground section of Frankfurt Station. We see its gleaming pristine white walls as they move.

PETER (*calls after her*): Do you know which city we're in? (*She continues walking.*) Which bloody city is this?

He glances round: the place is totally blank. He sees two fire buckets hanging on the wall, approaches one of them and tips it up. Frau Messner is not waiting, she continues walking sharply through the gleaming white passages.

Peter stares at the bottom of the fire bucket sees 'Frankfurt' printed on the bottom.

We're in Frankfurt. (*He calls after her.*) This is Frankfurt.

For a second he glances opposite him to where gleaming expensive goods, cameras and watches, are staring back out of a lighted shop window, and a photostat machine, lit by a blue light, revolves on a pedestal like a piano.

(*He turns. A sharp smile.*) Where've you gone?

He sees Frau Messner standing by a chocolate machine and moves up to her.

(*He smiles.*) You've had five minutes.

FRAU MESSNER. Have you got some money? We can get some chocolate.

PETER (*slight smile*): No — I haven't any.

Frau Messner drops some money into it and pulls surprisingly forcefully. The handle with the chocolate inside gets stuck half-way.

FRAU MESSNER. Of course it's stuck!

She starts digging at it with a key from her bag to try to dislodge it.

Can you hold this machine please?

PETER (*ironic smile*): This is the food you promised, is it!

He holds the machine and she tries to prise it open. She manages to dislodge very little chocolate.

FRAU MESSNER (*she eats it and hands him a piece*): Come on, we have time.

PETER. Where on earth are you leading me?

15. Exterior. Outside station. Night.

They come out of the underground area, the station looms in back of shot.

PETER. Where are you going?

She moves off sharply. He watches her go for a second, then follows her, with a slight smile. A wide shot of them crossing in front of neon signs in German.

16. Exterior. Streets. Night.

They move down an older street. A tram rattles past them. Frau Messner walks across the tram lines as Peter moves sharply up to her.

PETER. Come on! We've already walked too far from the station.

17. Exterior. Opera House. Night.

We cut to them in a high shot approaching the glass doors of the Opera.

18. Interior. Opera House. Night.

We cut inside the plush and dramatic foyer of the new Opera Building. A monumental wall and an unmistakably typical European arts complex, although from the first two shots of just foyers and cascades of metal gold clouds we could be in an airport.

PETER. What on earth are we doing here?

FRAU MESSNER. There is no time to eat in a proper restaurant.

We move across the foyer to where the buffet food has been cleared away.

The man behind the buffet immediately says, in German, that they have finished, that it is after the second interval, but Frau Messner answers in sharp German, asking to be given some food and a drink.

She turns to Peter.

They are trying not to give us food.

PETER (*staring out across the foyer*): Extraordinary place to come. God, I'm so hungry.

FRAU MESSNER. You can have a drink too. I will buy you one.

PETER. No thank you. Just some food. You're certain we have time? There can only be quarter of an hour.

Two tiny pieces of quiche lorraine are produced on large white china plates.

As this is happening Peter looks across the foyer. It is deserted except for a solitary young businessman looking very similar to Kellner in his dress and demeanour, who is standing leaning against the closed bar, looking at a briefcase of papers.

(*Peter glances across*): He looks like that businessman in our compartment. They seem to come out at this time of night. (*He smiles.*) Crawl out into the light.

By the bar there is an incongruous tank of tropical fish underneath a poster for the opera. Peter is staring into the tank with the glossy shiny fish swimming around. He smiles and turns to see Frau Messner holding two plates with the tiny portions of food on them.

FRAU MESSNER. Here.

She moves across the foyer, followed by Peter.

PETER (*crossing the foyer, looking about him*): Euro-splendour! (*A slight smile.*) Why's it so enormous?

As they move towards the leather chairs underneath the huge plate-glass windows, two security guards begin to gesticulate and shout at them in German. Frau Messner answers them back and then turns sharply.

FRAU MESSNER (*explaining*): You are not allowed to sit there unless you have tickets for the opera! And we have not. They are idiots. We will sit here then.

She sits underneath the plate-glass windows. The night lights of Frankfurt can be seen outside.

There is a close-circuit television near the stairs, mounted on the wall, showing the opera that is playing at the moment: the last act of 'Die Rosenkavalier' is flickering in black and white.

A large vase of artificial flowers sprouts out near the staircase.

Peter sits gingerly opposite her.

PETER. I'm going to keep a close check on the time.

He takes out his watch and puts it right next to him.

I don't think this is going to work! We can't possibly have time — we walked a long way from the station.

FRAU MESSNER. There is time. (*Nibbling her food.*) There is no need to worry.

PETER. You better be right. (*Slight smile.*) It's important to me — not that you're the slightest bit interested. You realise it's nearly midnight.

Shot of the security guards across the foyer locking some doors and standing waiting with a large bunch of keys.

(*Smiles.*) It's a strange feeling being away from the train, one feels one shouldn't be. (*Laconic smile.*) Like being out of school, it's forbidden and we'll

be spotted any moment. (*He stretches out his hand.*) At least the flowers on the train were real. (*He touches them.*) These are wax.

He glances at the opera on the television monitor. Music from the opera is audible.

He suddenly looks at her, sitting on the chair underneath the huge windows eating her food, sitting very still. She looks up and gives him a sharp stare.

Why are you so calm suddenly?

FRAU MESSNER (*on the bar stool*): It's my birthday you know, tomorrow.

PETER. Is it?

FRAU MESSNER. I still remember my birthday, the date, but not the number. (*She looks at him.*) I am not very well, I may be quite badly ill.

PETER. You look incredibly well to me.

FRAU MESSNER. I hope my flat will be clean when I get there — I cannot come back to a dirty flat.

Distant music starts very quietly drifting towards them.

PETER. Naturally.

FRAU MESSNER. During the war we lived in a much larger house of course, with its own grounds.

PETER. During the war . . . if you're like this now, what were you like then! You were probably a leading light of the *Party*!

FRAU MESSNER (*stares straight at him, focusing her eyes on him*): We lost all our servants of course. They left us! Except for one, he was very fat. His face was covered all in boils. He was useless. There was dirt everywhere! Even all over my bed. I don't know how we managed. We also had this nice young girl — but she disappeared one day. I don't know if she was Jewish, she may have been Jewish. (*She looks at him to see his reaction.*) Perhaps that's where she went. We didn't see her again.

PETER. You don't even know . . .

FRAU MESSNER. He had boils all over his face — the other man! I haven't thought about him for years, till tonight. My brothers were all in the Party, I think, most of them — I took no part. I didn't care for it really. In the shops they started to say 'Heil Hitler' instead of 'Grussgott' even when you just went in for a drink of coffee. Of course you don't know what it means, it is a very famous Austrian saying, 'When they came to Wien, the Germans, the Anschluss . . .' (*Peter quietly listening.*) When they came, everyone threw little dried mountain flowers in bundles, tied up with bows. They were all over the street the next morning as far as you could look. It was like a lake it was so deep. They covered your feet. I have still got some somewhere I think, put away. (*Pause.*) I didn't enjoy that time though.

PETER (*watching fascinated. Smiles*): Didn't you.

FRAU MESSNER. It is peculiar how one talks to strangers when one is on a train.

PETER. But we're not on a train!

FRAU MESSNER (*soothingly*): You will be again in a minute, you don't have to worry. I have never missed a train.

She sips her drink.

I was young you see then, quite young. I was used to all the dances and parties. (*She nibbles her small piece of food.*) And suddenly there were not so many parties. We still had some of course. The men all in uniform, they smelt more of smoke. We still had the Viennese complexion, all of us, the girls, it was very famous, a peach complexion, not brown like everybody is today — we kept it all through the war. I was alone of course for a lot of the time in the war. So I read. I read a lot of long books. In the afternoons. It was very quiet. By myself.

Music pouring out from the auditorium.

PETER. Why are you telling me this now?

FRAU MESSNER (*looking straight at him*): Because it interests me to see you listen. To watch you.

Pause. Peter looks back at her.

PETER. So, what have you found out about me then?

FRAU MESSNER (*shrewd look*): Are you . . . from Oxford or Cambridge?

PETER (*pauses, sharp smile*): Both.

FRAU MESSNER (*looking at the food*): Do you want some more? (*Indicating tiny pieces of food they have been eating.*) I think I must have some more now, bitte.

PETER (*leaning forward to restrain her*): No. You really are trying to make me miss the train. Aren't you?

FRAU MESSNER. Why should I do that?

PETER. Because it amuses you. Some sort of revenge.

FRAU MESSNER. What would I want revenge for?

PETER. For not getting your own way. Everything else may wait for you — but a trans-continental express is not going to.

FRAU MESSNER. There is plenty of time.

PETER (*loud*): It may not matter to you if you miss the train but it matters like hell to me. I have an important appointment.

FRAU MESSNER. Of course it's important.

Frau Messner finishes sorting out her change and stands up.

But there is plenty of time. I think I will just go in there to listen to the last act. They are reaching the trio — I remember Lotte Lehmann, I won't be a moment.

Frau Messner moves off across the foyer.

PETER (*looks at his watch*): Christ, I think my watch has stopped! What's the time?

He turns and rushes down the stairs. A receding shot of Frau Messner climbing the stairs and opening the door into the Circle as the ushers converge on her.

19. Interior. Staircase. Night.

As the music soars through the trio Peter plunges down the staircase and finds that he has come out in a different part of the ground floor.

He runs along the plate-glass windows and tries a door which is locked.

PETER. Locked the audience in! (*Muttering.*) How do you get out of this bloody place! (*Muttering, half-audible.*) Why don't they tell how to get out?

He runs back along the glass wall, past some more of the building's strange decor.

For a brief second he is trapped, unable to find his way out.

A wide shot of him moving along the great glass wall, and knocking over an ornamental ashtray, before he gets out into the street.

He smiles to himself, regaining his composure and begins to run, not a panicky run, but a fast, determined run through the night streets.

20. Exterior. Railway Station. Night.

A shot of Peter running across the tram lines with a tram rattling down them just behind him, past the giant poster, and plunging down the steps that lead to the whole underground area, where late night music is still playing.

He runs past the ageing hippy playing his guitar, who is still sitting against the wall, watching from the shadows, and across the concourse of the station,

having to step over some kids lying on the floor by the side-entrance. A girl is lying flat on her back, her arms spread out wide, staring upwards at the roof. A whistle is blowing loudly.

21. Exterior. Railway Station. Platform.

Peter arrives at the platform. The train has gone. He stands still in the middle of the concourse for a moment.

The sound of footsteps are ringing out − he turns and stares in the direction they are coming from.

Frau Messner appears, walking briskly into view. Her footsteps are echoing out in the late night atmosphere of the station. A look of controlled fury in Peter's eyes as he waits for her to get within range.

PETER (*when she reaches him, staring straight at her. Controlled fury breaking into rage*): I have missed the train. The train has gone.

She stands some distance away from him.

It − has − gone. You have got us stuck in this bloody city. You idiot, what the hell do you think you were doing?

Frau Messner just stares at him.

Do you realise you have made me miss the train?

FRAU MESSNER (*very still and calm*): It shouldn't have gone yet.

PETER (*controlled fury*): What do you mean it shouldn't − it has and I am stuck in this godforsaken place − with you.

They stand isolated in the centre of the platform watched by three kids.

You did this deliberately didn't you? (*He looks straight at her.*) You really are an evil old woman, do you know that.

A pause.

Frau Messner faces him.

*A big close-up: her face impassive,
just looking at him.*

Did you hear what I said?

FRAU MESSNER (*icily*): I heard you.

PETER (*shouting*): Well what are you
going to do about it then?

FRAU MESSNER (*staring back at him*):
There are people watching.

PETER. I don't care who's watching.
(*He shouts straight at her, more
dangerous.*) You have made me miss the
train.

*A high shot of them standing together
in the concourse, with the two
thirteen-year-old girls with very short
hair we saw earlier, staring at them
from against the wall with blank
expressions.*

So what am I going to do then?

FRAU MESSNER. You could take an
aeroplane.

PETER (*shouts*): At this time of *night*
— To Linz?

FRAU MESSNER. The train *should not*
have gone yet.

PETER. I told you it . . .

He is cut off by a whistle blowing.

*He turns and looks back across the
station. Through a gap between some
advertising hoardings he catches a
glimpse of a train.*

A look of total surprise on Peter's face.

FRAU MESSNER (*a slight smile*): The
train has not gone — it has moved to
another platform.

*He runs very fast across the station
— an athletic run. We keep close
to him, tracking very fast.*

*For an instant he falls on his stomach
on the edge of the puddle — we hear
the sound of a jacket ripping — but
he pulls himself up instantly, and runs
along the side of the train. He opens
the door and climbs in.*

*Frau Messner is yards and yards
behind him, refusing to run.*

The whistle blows.

We hear the noise of the engine.

She does not quicken her walk.

22. Interior. Train compartment. Night.

*Peter moves up to his compartment. His
suit is torn.*

*The compartment is full of strange
kids he has not seen before staring back
at him. The atmosphere is smoky. There
are beer cans all over the floor.*

PETER. The people who were in here
before. Where are they?

*A shot of the kids' faces, hostile and
sullen.*

DIETRICH. Have you had your supper?

PETER. There was a bag up here. Do
you know where it is? A brown bag.
What has happened to it?

*Suddenly, from the shadows, Dietrich
stretches out a hand.*

DIETRICH. And you think they've
taken it! Don't panic.

*He throws Peter's bag at him and
gives him a strange look.*

They are in the sleeping car. It's your
bedtime now. That way — go on. You'll
find her there. Shon gluck!

23. Interior. Train compartment. Night.

*Cut to the steward swinging the seats
over in the compartment and turning
them into beds.*

*Frau Messner is staring around her —
and at Peter. They are all standing in
the corridor, lined up against the wall,
except for Lorraine who is absent.*

*The small man is at the end of the
row. His face is impassive, his eyes
half-closed.*

The kids suddenly appear at the other end of the corridor, singing and shouting. Dietrich has drunk a lot. His manner is dangerously volatile. In a sudden flurry of action during Preston's following speech, a fight breaks out in the corridor, at first it is just rowdy play, with much abuse being shouted.

PRESTON. Bed time now! Not that we'll get much sleep, mind you, I can sleep through almost everything even babies crying and burglar alarms; but not the police sirens. (*He glances at the raucous kids.*) That's what they need now . . .

FRAU MESSNER (*glancing at Peter and then away again*): We can't all sleep in there can we? We won't fit.

KELLNER. We will have to. We will fit.

FRAU MESSNER (*glancing at Peter*): I think I would prefer to stand here all night.

PRESTON. It's all right once you're in bed. They leave you a sheet sleeping bag you see, and you make up your own bed.

FRAU MESSNER (*stops the steward loudly in English, so Peter can hear*): Can you just finish it? Make my bed for me.

The steward ignores her and slides back the door of the fat man's compartment. The fat man, is surrounded by empty seats.

FAT MAN. They're all in the dining car! they will be coming back soon!

PRESTON. You make your own bed you see.

He guides her into the compartment followed by the small man.

If you don't mind me saying so, you do speak very good English.

FRAU MESSNER. I know I do. I always have done, since I was a small girl.

Suddenly the fight erupts into something much more savage. Dietrich

takes on one of the other kids. There is a violent fight with a broken bottle and Dietrich gets his face slashed, badly cut. It is brief and sudden.*

Peter stares at the retreating figures of the kids, the sudden burst of manic energy has now gone and the corridor is quiet again.

We cut to Kellner staring out of the window. Peter is standing next to him.

KELLNER (*deeply agitated*): The train is going so slow. It is nearly two hours late now.

He smiles at Peter.

I have to be back in my office by seven o'clock in the morning. I should be on a plane, but we have a strike. I don't like being late. I don't know what is wrong with this train.

The train makes creaking noises.

PETER. It's falling to pieces.

KELLNER (*his nose up to the window, which is open to the outside blackness*): We are by a big river. There are villas down there. Huge new houses. Very, very rich people. All on top of each other, as far as you can see.

PETER (*his face to the black glass*): Out there?

KELLNER (*his manner suddenly very speedy*): I haven't slept for four days, and four nights!

PETER. You haven't?

Peter turns. Frau Messner is standing right behind him in the doorway of the compartment.

KELLNER. No. Been too busy, (*He smiles.*) making business. And tomorrow night I am meant to go to the opera — it's my one pleasure. We have an enormous new opera house. Yes, the stage is the size of an oil tanker. (*His hand is drumming on the window sill.*) It is going too slowly, we will never get there, what is wrong? I don't know why it is moving like this.

Kellner retreats to his bunk.

Lorraine appears in the corridor.

PETER. There you are!

LORRAINE (*looking at his muddy suit*): What happened to you at supper?

PETER. I've been looking for you!

LORRAINE. I can't find anywhere here, to do my toilet. They're all occupied.

PETER. Can't you? (*He glances over his shoulder at Frau Messner.*) Come with me — I'll show you where.

Peter takes Lorraine's hand and pulls her along the corridor, past the band of kids grouped together drinking, their aggressive drunken faces looking at them as they pass. There are cans all over the floor.

(*Quite aggressive.*) You're going to the Gents!

He pulls open the door of the Gents, which is not locked.

Dietrich looks up, his mouth and chin are covered in blood. He is spitting out blood into the basin.

DIETRICH. Why don't you come in?

They both look startled as he bends over the basin, lifting cold water up to his cut mouth and splashing it on, seemingly oblivious to the pain.

He indicates the blood and water in the basin.

Nice colour — don't you think? (*He smiles.*) Nice to swim in there.

He reaches out to his jacket which is on the lavatory seat and puts it on.

Did I show you my photos?

Dietrich gives them a sharp, intelligent, piercing look, and drops the photographs one by one, into the basin, so that they are floating on the water.

How do you say — family snaps. (*He grins.*) and photos of me doing things that aren't allowed. Verboten!

He tosses the others down the lavatory, grinning, and saying something in German.

He moves past them. He gives them a charming lewd smile.

If you go to the first class, the toilets are much bigger, much more room.

PETER. Come on — go in there.

LORRAINE (*surprised by his aggression*): Thank you. Aren't you going to shut the door?

PETER. No, we're leaving it open. I'll stand guard. I want to talk to you.

Lorraine washes the blood out of the basin. She lifts the photographs out of the basin and drops them on the floor.

Why the hell did you give her your dinner ticket?

LORRAINE. Because she wanted it.

Peter watches Lorraine through the door.

Lorraine rolls up her sleeve. She is very brown, with long brown legs.

PETER. Is this a conspiracy of yours? You realise I was nearly left stranded in that station because of you?

LORRAINE. You're still here aren't you?

PETER. For the moment.

Frau Messner is standing in the corridor.

Peter can see her.

LORRAINE. She doesn't mean you any harm you know.

PETER. Oh really! (*A slight smile.*) I don't feel safe I really don't.

He looks down the corridor.

Frau Messner is standing quite close in the corridor, glancing towards him and then away.

(*A slight grin.*) God, she's still watching me.

LORRAINE (*looking straight at him*): You don't get much privacy on trains.

PETER. No. (*Giving her a gentle tug.*)
Come on this way.

LORRAINE. Where are we going?

PETER. Where she's not watching.

*He tugs her gently down the corridors
of the train. They have to pick their
way over the sleeping kids: eyes shut,
young faces lying crammed up
together in the corridor.*

24. Interior. Train. Dining car. Night.

*Peter and Lorraine approach the dining
car door. Peter opens the door. From
their point of view we see the whole
dining car piled up with sleeping kids, on
tables and on chairs, or hunched up,
sitting on tables and leaning against
windows. Most of them are asleep though
occasionally they murmur or turn over.
One very young girl is sitting propped up
against the window. They sit next to her.*

LORRAINE (*on seeing the crowded
carriage*): God!

PETER. Well we're sort of alone. (*With
a charming smile. He looks at the kids
asleep with their belongings all around
him. They find a space in the crowded
carriage.*) When I was young all I ever
wanted to do was live on trains —
literally. Have my own compartment
and eat and sleep, criss-cross Europe and
fall in love and write about what I saw
outside the window. And never get off
when it stopped, and become famous
of course.

*While Lorraine says the following
lines she moves the head of the
sleeping girl on the table slightly so
that there's more room.*

LORRAINE. Do you really want success?
Well maybe this is the beginning for you
tonight.

PETER (*smiles a sympathetic smile*): Of
course, in a way. I'm not obsessed
about it, I don't lust after it in corners,

but I quite like it. I never believe anybody
that says otherwise, especially now. It's
a very competitive time.

A shot of the sleeping kids.

*A shot of Lorraine with the night
lights outside the window passing
across her face. Her long brown arms
stretched out on the table.*

LORRAINE (*sharp*): I wish you luck.
I hope you manage it.

*Peter stares at her, uncertain what she
means.*

*As she sits by the window her
bodly clearly visible, he moves nearer
to her.*

*Raucous singing is still audible from
down the train.*

PETER. Sometimes one meets people
on trains — talks to them for hours, and
then they're gone and you never even
found out their names.

LORRAINE. You haven't asked me.
(*Straight at him.*) My name's Lorraine.

PETER (*staring at her*): Why are you
so brown? How did you manage it?

LORRAINE (*looking down at her arms*):
It's coming off fast — ever since I
arrived over here. (*She looks up at him.
A sharp, intelligent look.*) I hated
England. It gave me the creeps. (*Looks
at him.*) To be crude. And Europe gives
me the creeps to.

PETER. That's ridiculous. You've only
just arrived.

LORRAINE. That's right. It's
extraordinary but I already want to go
home. I can't wait to get back. I will
be counting the days, I can feel it now.
(*A slight smile.*) Notching them up on
the hotel wall. We Americans are meant
to find it so amazing over here — aren't
we? (*Straight at him.*) But I don't.
(*Staring at him, speaking with surprising
force.*) The atmosphere here is so ugly.

PETER (*a slight smile at her*): And that
includes the people you've met does it?

LORRAINE (*staring straight at him*):
Very definitely.

PETER (*startled*): All of them?

LORRAINE (*still looking at him*): Yes,
most of them. I just really don't like it.
I hate it.

*We feel the real darkness of her mood
as the lights play across her face. Peter
stares at her, sensing the darkness of
her mood but unable to say anything.
She looks straight at him.*

I'd better go.

She leaves the dining car.

25. Interior. Train compartment. Night.

*Cut to inside the compartment with all
of them lying in their bunks, except for
Peter, who slides back the door and
enters.*
  *Lorraine is not there. He stands by
the door and enters. As he does so the
shouting and singing wafts in from the
passage. The train is creaking.*

PETER. Which is my bunk?

FRAU MESSNER (*sharp*): Here.

PETER (*quiet*): Opposite you.

*His is the second bunk up, level with
Frau Messner's.*

*Peter taking his shirt off, moving to
his bunk.*

I see you've had your bunk made for
you!

FRAU MESSNER. We must stop that
noise, that terrible noise.

*The noise from the passage is getting
increasingly loud.*

PRESTON (*who is in the bottom
bunk*): We can have some music.

*Preston moves to the panel above the
door.*

PETER. There's a radio here?

PRESTON. Yes. (*Flicking the wall

switch. 'Puppet On a String'
bounces out.*) This won the Eurovision
song contest – they always play their
old winners here on this.

*Peter switches out the light and
climbs into bed. He is bare-chested,
still wearing mud-spattered trousers.
He lies on top of the sheets, his face
very close to Frau Messner's*

*The music creaks into Beethoven's
Sixth Symphony.*

*The only light is the blue night-light
in the ceiling which is flickering badly.*

We go past all the heavy industry in
Germany soon. Thousands of acres of it –
it makes a noise too.

FRAU MESSNER. It is so ugly. It's no
wonder some young people try to blow
it up – anarchists.

PETER (*looking across to her face, which
is very close*): You're not going to talk
all night – are you? Please just try to
make an effort and be quiet for a bit can
you?

FRAU MESSNER (*a moment's pause.
She stares back at him impassively*): I
will not be able to sleep with that light
flickering like that.

PETER. Of course you can.

FRAU MESSNER. Will you just take it
out for me? Reach up and take it out.

PETER (*angry, hesitates for a second,
then getting out of bed and reaching up
to the blue light*): This is probably
dangerous, it may stop the whole train.

*He reaches for the light. It is hot.
He takes it out and puts the bulb on
the end of his bed.*

*The compartment goes into total
darkness except for a little light from
the window.*

*Peter glances out into the corridor. At
the far end he can see Lorraine standing
by herself, staring out of the window.
A solitary image. He watches her for
a second.*

(*Calls out.*) See you in the morning.

Lorraine does not react.

Peter moves back into the compartment.

For a moment we stay on Lorraine. She is leaning her head against the window, staring out.

Peter lies down again.

Frau Messner is still staring at him – a hard stare.

PRESTON (*flicking off the music and lying back*): My name is Preston. I live in Maidstone, and soon I'll be where no one can find me. Goodnight!

For a moment outside the window there is a noise of heavy industry. The sound of a whole plant working. Lights shine through the blinds, terribly bright and then are gone.

Outside in the corridor we hear Dietrich singing an American song, half in German and half in English, really raucous and out of tune.

Peter's eyes half close. He opens them. Frau Messner is still staring at him.

He closes his eyes.

A close up of Frau Messner's eyes as kids shout in the passage.

Dissolve on Peter's face. The soundtrack changes. He half opens his eyes. Frau Messner is still staring her impassive stare.

Dissolve on Peter's face. He opens his eyes.

Her bunk is empty. She is standing in the doorway, her back to the compartment. Peter closes his eyes.

Montage of vivid night-shots: of cars moving in the night, as seen from the train, and the industrial landscape, floodlit and vast.

The screen goes black for a split second and then a German voice shouts something inaudible and a torch flashes straight into Peter's eyes.

FIRST GUARD. Passport. Passport.

Two torches shine in his face. The noise of the train is deafeningly loud for a moment as he wakes up.

Peter's point of view as two German Border guards stare down.

Passport.

Peter sleepily reaches for his passport. The guards are looking down at him. They glance at the passport and look back at him. The first guard's torch wanders down his mud-spattered trousers.

Where did you get on the train please?

PETER. Ostend.

FIRST GUARD. Your ticket.

Peter searches his mud-covered jacket. His eyes clogged with sleep. The torches shine on him, there is no other light.

PETER. It must have fallen out when I fell over, but it has been clipped about ten times already. I had to run for the train.

FIRST GUARD (*shining the torch down his body*): Could you come out in the passage please.

PETER. What now?

Peter puts his jacket round his bare chest and goes out into the passage.

There is no light in the passage, only the light from the torches. It is still night outside.

FIRST GUARD. Are you English?

PETER (*more awake now*): You've seen my passport.

FIRST GUARD. And where is your ticket?

PETER. I hope I won't have to say everything four times. I dropped it.

FIRST GUARD. Why have you got mud all over your clothes?

PETER (*smiles*): That's hardly an offence, is it?

FIRST GUARD. I asked you a question sir.

PETER (*surprised*): Sir? I fell over – running for a train in Frankfurt.

FIRST GUARD (*sharp*): I thought you said you got on this train at Ostend?

PETER. I did. Yes. But I was coaxed off it, against my better judgement by another passenger, in Frankfurt.

Peter stares back at the two guards who have their torches trained on him.

The first guard is a handsome man of about thirty, quite tall, with piercing eyes.

FIRST GUARD. Why have you got mud all over your trousers.

PETER (*much sharper*): You've just asked me that question! The answer's the same. (*Very slowly.*) I *fell* onto the ground. Into a large puddle to be precise. Splash. I had to run because she'd made me late.

They watch him.

Look, ask any of the passengers in there. They all saw me get on.

He points back into the compartment, they shine their torches. The light flicks from bunk to bunk. They are all empty.

(*Really surprised.*) Where have they all gone? They must have got out in Munich.

The torch lights come to rest on the top bunk. The small man is still there asleep, his body bunched up.

He's still here! Wake up! Come on, wake up!

The torch light is trained full on the small man's face but he is absolutely oblivious.

He didn't see me get on at Ostend, but he'll do. Wake up!

He shakes the small man who stirs very slightly, but only to start breathing heavily again.

God he's a heavy sleeper. He's almost in a coma. *Wake up.*

FIRST GUARD. Come here.

Peter moves towards them.

(*His tone very sharp now.*) We are going to have to search you please.

PETER. Going to search me?

FIRST GUARD. Just turn around. No round like that. Put your hands up there.

They search him, quite politely.

They make him face the wall.

PETER (*nervous smile*): You've already done it once in this carriage – isn't this victimisation? No, that was in Belgium wasn't it?

He sees out of the corner of his eye the second guard looking through a glossy catalogue with photos in it, looking at the page and then at Peter.

What's he doing?

FIRST GUARD. He's looking you up.

PETER. What is it – a glossy brochure of terrorists. Do I look like a terrorist?

FIRST GUARD. We have to check. It is very easy for people to jump trains and get out of Germany, people who shouldn't be leaving.

PETER. But I'm English.

FIRST GUARD. A lot of them speak very good English. They are educated and well dressed. (*Standing close to him.*) Some person fused all the lights in this part of the train. Do you know about that?

PETER. No.

FIRST GUARD. You sure you know nothing about that?

PETER (*suddenly glances over his shoulder to his bunk where the light bulb is lying*): No I don't. (*Loud.*) This journey is becoming a bloody assault course! And it's beginning to get beyond a joke, I'm going back to bed now, OK?

FIRST GUARD (*stops him, holding his arm*): I'm afraid not.

The second guard has gone into the compartment and is idly shining his torch around. Peter is watching out of the corner of his eye.

You're sure you can't tell us anything more about this mud? That you say you got in Frankfurt Station!

PETER. God you're really paranoid about this aren't you? (*He flicks at the mud, his voice rising, trying to smile.*) I don't want to be rude, but you are, under international law, allowed on a train wearing mud!

The second guard walks out of the compartment. The first guard turns. They have found the light on his bed.

FIRST GUARD. There is the light. You fused the whole carriage. Why?

PETER (*loud*): I took that bulb out because *she* asked me to. Because it wasn't working properly.

FIRST GUARD (*slowly*): We are going to take you off the train now. We will check your name on our computer.

PETER (*really nervous and excited*): Your computer! What computer, for Chrissake?

FIRST GUARD. And then we will charge you for this offence. Interfering with train property.

PETER (*disbelief*): You're going to take me off this train? Listen I've got to be somewhere tomorrow, can't I report there . . . or . . .

FIRST GUARD. No, you must come now. With us.

The train is beginning to slow down.

PETER. Where you taking me?

FIRST GUARD. We will have to drive you thirty kilometers.

PETER. Thirty kilometers! To some remote police station. (*Very nervous and excited.*) I'm sorry to labour the point but I *am English*, and although we are members of the Community, I hardly think that entitles you to take me off at four in the morning, just because I have mud on my trousers and removed a faulty light bulb.

He looks at them.

FIRST GUARD. We are arresting you, come now.

PETER. For Chrissake if I was a terrorist I would have shot you five minutes ago.

The guard tenses.

This is insane, you can't be that stupid — don't you understand — *she* asked me to remove the light bulb, the old woman, she . . . (*Suddenly the thought hits him.*) But she's still on the train of course, she was going to Vienna. (*He looks at them.*) She's on this train, we must find her.

He moves off down the corridor. The second guard lunges for him, violently, and grabs him roughly from behind. The light of the torches is stabbing everywhere.

They stop opposite a ladies lavatory. Peter is looking shaken.

He stares down at the door and sees that the lavatory is engaged.

The train has stopped.

It's probably her.

FIRST GUARD. You have to come now.

PETER (*calls at the door*): Come on, come out. I need you out here.

He bangs on the door.

Come *out here*!

The door opens and a small girl emerges, blinking in the light of the torch and looking frightened.

Peter glances up at the guard.

That's not her. (*Then he suddenly realises he has seen the girl at the beginning of the journey.*) She saw me. In Ostend. Come on you remember, I saw you! (*Loud.*) Don't you remember?

The girl looks afraid and runs away.

FIRST GUARD (*taking him very firmly by the arm*): Come this way please. We cannot hold up the train, it is very late as it is! We will take your luggage.

The second guard is holding his case.

Put on your shoes. Do you want to wear your shoes?

Peter, looking dazed, begins to put on his shoes and socks.

Quickly the train is waiting.

26. Exterior. Police cars. Night.

We cut to outside the train which has stopped.

The two policemen lead him over to where a police car is waiting.

Further away a larger police van is standing, its headlights shining. The door of the police car is opened and his belongings, which have now been put in a plastic bag, are thrown inside.

There are suddenly several more police talking in German. They are near a huge industrial building which shoots into the sky.

The lighted train stands still. People peer from its windows.

The younger guard is standing a few paces away by the car, covering him, his hand on his gun.

The first guard has leant into the car and is talking – in rapid German – on a police radio. Occasionally he smiles, chatting away on the radio, glancing over in Peter's direction.

FIRST GUARD. We are just checking where we have to take you.

The large police van starts up and moves off on to the road where it waits, its lights flashing.

The noise and lights from the industrial complex are harsh and loud.

Peter is now getting more and more nervous. He looks very pale.

Two workmen are sitting watching – listening to a transistor radio – and staring at him. A jaunty, ridiculous song is playing on the radio.

Peter glances at the young guard who looks seemingly sympathetically towards him and moves up to him.

SECOND GUARD. Cigarette?

He gives it to Peter whose hand is shaking.

PETER. Listen. (*Nervous smile.*) Look, I have a letter explaining the purpose of my visit and . . .

He takes out his wallet. The young guard glances down at the wallet. Peter notices this. The guard is looking down, seemingly interested in the money. Peter glances up at the guard's young face.

Would you – I mean this isn't a bribe, I mean this is probably (*He swallows.*) rather idiotic of me, but if I gave you that (*He takes out a hundred marks.*) would you just take me back on the train – just for a moment, to look for the old lady, because she'll explain, she'll . . .

The young guard looks down at the note, takes it from Peter. For a second Peter looks relieved.

Suddenly the young guard is shouting violently, calling over another young policeman who is standing nearby. A loud sharp shout. They both suddenly pin Peter up against the car, very violently, as they frisk him quite viciously, shouting in German at him. They do not hit him, but swing him round several times, frisking him all over, violently, so that his body is pounded against the car, his head going down against the metal.

The young guard is furious. He pulls Peter's arm round and bundles him into the car, where he sits very badly shaken and bruised.

The first guard moves over calling sharply to the young guard who starts explaining in German. They shine torches through the window at him.

For a moment Peter sits dazed on the back seat, leaning his head against the window as the police move all around. The indicator is blinking on the dashboard and the noise from the car radio is stabbing out.

He glances down at the seat beside him. The light bulb he removed from the compartment is lying neatly wrapped up in a transparent bag next to him. He stares at it for a moment, then at the mud on his trousers in disbelief.

Suddenly the car is full of police. They sit close to him, holding on to him.

(*very quiet.*) Where are you taking me?

The car starts off, its siren going. It reverses violently.

Peter stares back at the train. A few people, none of whom he recognizes, are staring out of the lighted windows, fascinated, craning to get a better look.

Somebody takes a photograph with a flashlight.

The car swings round and begins to drive along the road.

Peter glances behind him. The large police car is tracking them, its siren also on, its headlights blazing towards him.

A police motorcyclist roars off in the opposite direction.

(*Very quiet.*) Please . . . could you just let me explain again . . .

His hand goes nervously up to his mouth.

None of them are looking at him, he sinks back in his seat, his face very pale.

The cars are moving long the waiting train. Suddenly in the car headlights, in the middle of the road, Frau Messner is standing.

For a moment it looks as if she is alone in the middle of the road, and then we see she is with one of the train guards.

The car brakes suddenly. Frau Messner remains some distance from the car while the two policemen in the front seats get out and move over to her.

She talks rapidly to them in German, loud, authoritative tones: 'The boy is with me' etc. They glance back towards Peter after a pause.

The first guard who arrested him on the train moves back to the car, and opens the door. He looks down at Peter.

FIRST GUARD. You were correct. What you told us is correct. Please rejoin the train.

They hand him his belongings. Frau Messner has climbed aboard the train.

Peter moves towards the train, still looking very shaken. People are leaning out of the window, staring at him in fascinated silence as he gets onto the train.

He leans exhausted against the window as the train moves off. There are bruises on his head, he flinches in pain. He is momentarily totally shattered.

27. Interior. Train. Corridor. Dawn.

Frau Messner is standing in the empty corridor looking across at him. For a moment there is silence.

FRAU MESSNER. I have sent them away now.

PETER (*still speeding with nerves*): Where the hell were you?

FRAU MESSNER. I went for a little walk.

They are standing by the join between the two carriages. Light is coming from the other carriage, through the doors, and the dawn light is coming up.

You were lucky I came back.

PETER. I was *lucky.* You realise this is

all your fault. I am covered in mud which is apparently a capital offence in this country, I have committed a crime with a light bulb, and I have lost my rail ticket.

FRAU MESSNER (*rubs at the mud on his sleeve. He has his jacket draped round his bare shoulders*): The mud will come off.

PETER. Don't touch me! (*Pause.*) I was taken off the train because of you. I was arrested because *you* asked me . . .

FRAU MESSNER. You should have been more careful. You shouldn't look suspicious, behave suspiciously, they are looking for that.

PETER (*furious*): Behave suspiciously?

FRAU MESSNER. You should realise these things. (*Pause.*) Now maybe we can put the beds back. It's nearly morning, it's impossible to sleep now. (*Pointedly.*) Could you come and put the beds back because they are heavy . . .

PETER (*exploding*): Christ, I've just had about *all I can take from you*. (*Really shouting.*) You realise you have ruined my journey. You have constantly pestered and provoked and jabbered at me.

He suddenly grabs hold of her arm and shakes her violently backwards and forwards in the doorway as the train begins to pick up speed.

(*Shaking her, holding on to her very tightly.*) I will *not* do anything more for you. You understand? Not a single thing more. *Leave me alone. Will you just leave me alone now. Right! And don't come anywhere near me again.* Do you understand that. (*Screams.*) *Just leave me alone!*

As he really shakes her body her head goes back as if expecting to be hit. Peter lets go of her. They are standing in the doorway. She stares back at him, her face showing no emotion. Peter looks slightly shocked at what he has done. He looks away

for a second and then at her face. She turns abruptly and goes away through the doors into the other carriage.

28. Interior. Train compartment. Dawn.

Peter sits in the compartment. Dawn light is coming up.
Cut outside into the passage with the beer cans rolling up and down the corridor as the train really begins to travel furiously fast.
Cut back to Peter putting his shirt on. A close-up of him as he looks up, startled.
The bottom bunk is covered in silver paper, and one chicken leg is visible.

PETER (*rather startled*): Preston . . .

He stands up – his shirt still undone, but wearing his jacket – grabs his case and moves out into the corridor.

The fat man looks up from his empty compartment. The door to his compartment is open.

(*Looking at the empty bunks.*) Yes I know, they're in the dining car.

FAT MAN. Sssh. They're sleeping.

He is pointing at the cases he has pushed into the bunks to make them look like sleeping bodies.

Peter moves down the train, which is filled with early morning light.

As he passes, he sees a bundled shape lying stretched out in an empty compartment.

He opens the door. It is Dietrich. He is lying asleep on top of some magazines, looking very young.

He looks up at Peter for a second and turns towards the wall again, his cut face very noticeable in the morning light.

DIETRICH (*sounding quiet*): I have missed my stop. I was asleep. (*A slight grin.*) Too much beer!

PETER. Where are you going then?

DIETRICH. I don't know. Wherever I wake up.

The boy nestles up to the wall again.

Peter smiles slightly and moves on.

In the passage Peter stares around him, then moves fast, looking for Frau Messner.

PETER (*smiling to himself*): Where is she?

29. Interior. Corridors. Dawn.

Peter walks briskly down the train, through the other carriage which is almost empty now and through the empty bar, with its drinks locked away.

30. Interior. Train. Dining Car. Morning.

Peter walks into the dining car, with the early morning light filtering into it.

Frau Messner is sitting alone at the same table as before, as if expecting to be served. There is nobody else in the carriage.

The floor is covered in carnations. Vases have been knocked over and spilt, sweet papers and cigarettes are littered over the floor.

Frau Messner looks up. Peter stands in the doorway for a second, looking at her, winding the silver paper round his fingers.

PETER (*gazing around the carriage*): Did *you* make all this mess?

FRAU MESSNER (*taking him literally*): No — it was here already.

PETER (*comes up to the table and stands over her*): I thought I'd find you here, you look very at home, here. (*He moves the vase of flowers.*) It was Preston who took your sandwiches — the one that was nice to you. Not me.

FRAU MESSNER. It doesn't surprise me.

PETER. I've come to say goodbye. My stop is in five minutes.

FRAU MESSNER. You must get ready.

PETER. I am ready.

His shirt is open but he is holding his case.

FRAU MESSNER. I am very thirsty.

PETER (*leaning up to her*): When we arrive at my station I am *not*, I repeat not, going to fetch you a drink from the platform, and then get trapped here on this train bringing it back to you. (*Quietly.*) I can just see you fussing for your change as the train pulls out.

Pause.

FRAU MESSNER (*sharp*): I *am* thirsty now.

The train is rattling very fast.

There's an orange over there behind the fence, if you could . . .

Where the food was the night before a metal grid has been lowered, an orange is rolling backwards and forwards behind it. There is a gap in the wire.

Peter hesitates and then moves up to wire. He stretches his hand through the wire which has jagged edges.

PETER. You realise if the train jolts, I could rip my hand open.

He stretches for the orange and reaches it. He pulls it back through the hole.

There, one orange.

He drops it in front of her.

You're going to peel it for yourself.

He stares down at her in the early morning light.

You *can* peel an orange?

FRAU MESSNER. Of course. (*She looks around.*) But I usually have a knife.

PETER (*watching her try very gingerly to peel the orange*): You are extraordinary — like a member of a nearly extinct species. One of its last. You need a whole army of people to run around for you, before you even begin to function. A dying breed aren't you?

FRAU MESSNER. And you? I wonder how long you'll last? You didn't manage very well last night.

PETER (*stares at her*): I'll be OK.

FRAU MESSNER (*looks up*): You haven't shaved.

PETER. No, I haven't.

She looks at his shirt and bare chest. The bruises are still visible from the beating the police gave him.

FRAU MESSNER. And do your shirt up.

PETER. In a moment.

Peter fastens his cuffs.

FRAU MESSNER (*her tone changing*): It is my birthday today.

PETER. You told me.

FRAU MESSNER (*for his benefit*): I won't be travelling much more now. I am not very well. I most probably will be dead quite soon. In a year or so. I won't be here much longer.

PETER. Now don't start getting maudlin. It doesn't suit you. You're not really at all like that.

FRAU MESSNER (*blunt*): I was always spoilt. Always. (*She looks at him.*) We're rather alike in many ways you know.

PETER (*looks at her*): You're taking ages over that orange.

FRAU MESSNER (*pushing it across to him*): You can finish it for me now.

The train is beginning to brake. Frau Messner watches Peter standing in front of her, peeling the orange. He smiles at her.

Have you ever been to Vienna.

PETER. No.

FRAU MESSNER. You should have. You really must. You should see the Spanish Riding School, it is very famous, and the Grinzing, very famous Austrian wine gardens.

PETER. Yes.

FRAU MESSNER (*a shrewd look at him and then away*): Of course you could come today if you wished. I don't mind. I have a large flat. There are many rooms.

PETER (*involuntary smile*): I don't think I heard you.

FRAU MESSNER. Yes you heard me.

PETER. Come to Vienna with you!

FRAU MESSNER. If you wished.

PETER (*unable to resist*): Why?

FRAU MESSNER (*looking back into his blue eyes – a strong look*): Because I wish it.

Peter smiles. There is a moment's pause as their eyes meet.

PETER (*quietly*): Do you often ask men on trains home with you?

FRAU MESSNER (*looking past him*): I didn't hear what you said.

The train brakes.

I don't mind if you come or not.

He is looking down at her. The light is on his hair.

You should see Vienna.

PETER. It's very kind of you . . . but I can't I'm afraid, my work. I have to go and . . .

FRAU MESSNER. Of course. Your important work.

She looks away. He smiles to himself.

Why you smiling at me?

PETER. I wasn't.

FRAU MESSNER. You're lying. You were smiling in that way you have. I know what it means. I don't like your smile very much.

A pause.

She looks directly at him, the train is really braking.

PETER. I must say goodbye now.

FRAU MESSNER. Yes, go on then.

PETER. Maybe — (*A nervous smile as she looks at him.*)

We'll catch the same train again sometime.

He moves slightly towards the door. She turns away, but then looks up. as he nears the door.

FRAU MESSNER (*her tone is very precise*): You're a nice boy in many ways.

Peter stops.

You're good looking. You're quite clever. You notice things. And you're not at all cruel. (*She suddenly looks directly at him, then louder.*) But you don't care.

The train has stopped.

You pretend to of course, you pretend.

She is staring straight at him.

But you don't really care about anything do you?

She stares at his pale young face, as he stands holding his case.

Except maybe success in your work. Becoming very successful. It's all you have. You don't *feel* anything else. *Nothing. You just cannot feel anything else.*

She looks at him.

Can you?

Silence.

I wonder what will happen to you?

Peter is staring at the train door, looking bewildered.

(*Matter of fact.*) You can go now. The train has stopped.

She turns away. She is quite calm, she does not look at him.

Silence.

A noise of train doors banging.

PETER. Frau Messner?

She does not react.

He goes up to her. As he gets up to her she closes her eyes.

Frau Messner?

Silence.

She does not look up. Her eyes are shut. Peter, staring down at her, moves as if to touch her face. Her eyes open.

He immediately moves back.

She closes her eyes again.

He stands for a moment, unsure of what to do.

She is sitting back, her eyes closed, her face expressionless.

Goodbye then. (*He moves towards the door.*) This is my station.

He is by the door. She has closed her eyes again, she does not look at him.

(*Sharp.*) Aren't you going to say goodbye?

She does not look at him.

(*Sharper.*) Aren't you going to say goodbye then?

Silence.

He half moves.

Do you want to know my name?

Silence.

She is looking out of the window.

(*Louder, more urgent, angry.*) Don't you want to know my name?

31. Exterior. Station. Morning.

Cut to Peter walking along by blank, white walls. We stay close to his face. He looks shaken, dazed, a little lost for a moment. We stay on him as he passes more white walls and puts his case on a luggage and passenger moving pavement. His case moves away from him, down the pavement. He watches it go for a second and then climbs on the moving pavement, and with his back away from the camera, he slowly recedes along it, out of view.

Methuen's New Theatrescripts

Michael Abbensetts	*Samba*
Andrey Amalrik	*East-West & Is Uncle Jack a Conformist?*
Howard Brenton	*Sore Throats & Sonnets of Love and Opposition*
	Thirteenth Night & A Short Sharp Shock! (A Short Sharp Shock! written with Tony Howard)
David Cregan	*Poor Tom & Tina*
David Edgar	*Wreckers*
	Teendreams
David Halliwell	*The House*
Barrie Keefe	*Frozen Assets*
	Sus
	Bastard Angel
David Lan	*Sergeant Ola and his Followers*
John Mackendrick	*Lavender Blue & Noli Me Tangere*
David Mamet	*American Buffalo, Sexual Perversity in Chicago & Duck Variations*
Tony Marchant	*Thick as Thieves*
Mustapha Matura	*Nice, Rum an' Coca Cola & Welcome Home Jacko*
	Play Mas, Independence & Meetings
Michael Meyer	*Lunatic and Lover*
Stephen Poliakoff	*Strawberry Fields*
	Shout Across the River
	American Days
	The Summer Party
Dennis Potter	*Brimstone and Treacle*
C.P. Taylor	*Good*
Peter Whelan	*The Accrington Pals*
Nigel Williams	*Sugar and Spice & Trial Run*
Charles Wood	*Has 'Washington' Legs? & Dingo*

Also from Methuen:

Royal Court Writers Series

Anton Chekhov	*The Seagull*
	(A new version by Thomas Kilroy)
Paul Kember	*Not Quite Jerusalem*
Hanif Kureishi	*Borderline*
Stephen Lowe	*Tibetan Inroads*
	Touched
G.F. Newman	*Operation Bad Apple*

Royal Shakespeare Company Pit Playtexts

Peter Flannery	*Our Friends in the North*
Henrik Ibsen	*A Doll's House*
	(translated by Michael Meyer)
Edward Bulwer Lytton	*Money*

For a full list of plays and theatre books published by Methuen please write to:

Methuen London Ltd
Marketing Department (Drama)
North Way
Andover
Hampshire
SP10 5BE